FERNWEH

The Longing for Places Unknown

The Life Story

of

Peter Werner Kreuziger

Edited by Candy Christensen-Barker and Lil Barcaski

Published by: GWN Publishing

Cover Design: Kristina Conatser Captured by KC Design

Photos of the author: Pepito Masterpiece Portraits

ISBN: 978-1-959608-45-5

DEDICATION

To my honey bunnies, Mary, Courtney, and Casey. The journey would not have been as wonderful without each of you.

TABLE OF CONTENTS

MY FERNWEH BECOMES A REALITY, 15

BUILDING BUSINESSES & LASTING RELATIONSHIPS, 65

MY WORLD CRUISE, 191

FOREWORD

I am a third-generation Italian American immigrant on my mother's side. My life experience taught me to be sympathetic to the immigrant plight and lifestyle. I learned from a young age that the American Dream was true in my family: work hard and you can improve your life and the lives of your family members.

This isn't a popular ideal in today's cultural and political environment. One side of the country villainizes the immigrant population and the other tends to infantilize them. I've noticed that the way to change a person's perspective on these types of topics is to share stories, and that's why I'm excited that Peter is sharing his story in this book.

My friend Peter knows hospitality. The first time we went to lunch, he hosted me at his restaurant, Bon Appétit in Dunedin, Florida. Peter ordered a large seafood tower as our appetizer. After that decadent appetizer, I went light for lunch, ordering the Achieva 1942 salad. The Swiss cheese and Genoa salami and hard-boiled egg over mixed greens, topped with Garlic Burgundy Vinaigrette is something to be remembered. I raved over the salad as Peter told me his story.

By the time my plate was empty, I said, "My friend, you really should write a book. Your life story is a classic example of the American success story and people need to hear it!"

Peter has impeccable taste, and not just for edibles. His restaurants are top-notch in service, décor, atmosphere and fare. He has spent his career going above and beyond in order to provide the best possible experience for his guests. Most of all though, his story is one of inspirational ingenuity, grit, and determination. He has worked hard for all he has, and his is a story of the success of the American Dream. I know the sharing of his story will encourage others as it has me.

Gary Regoli, *CEO, Achieva Credit Union*

TESTIMONIALS

I have known Peter for over 30 years. He is a good friend with great business skills and an amazing life story.

Maureen "Moe" Freaney
City Commissioner, Dunedin, Florida

I have had the good fortune to personally experience hearing stories being told by Peter Kreuziger. Many times, he has had me completely engaged and on the edge of my seat in anticipation when listening to the stories of his school years, his travels, his family and friends, his businesses and other life experiences. Peter has certainly crafted the art of storytelling. Peter's next step in his journey of writing his autobiography seems like a natural extension of his keen ability to engage listeners and now readers with his written story.

London L. Bates
Attorney, Dunedin, Florida resident

As Peter's Spiritual advisor and friend, I have admired the fact that his employees affectionately identify him as Mr. K. because he states he is in the Happiness Business, a wonderful way to look at life. This good man has enjoyed an eclectic life, which he shares in his memoir. Peter is a true giver in life.

Robert "Bob" Swick
Rev. Pastor, Veterans Advocate
St. Francis of Assisi Old Catholic Church, Dunedin

I have known Peter K. for 33 years. I have worked for a Fortune 100 company, have owned my own company and feel that Peter is an understanding business leader and a wonderful supporter of, and has played a significant role in, the development and success of the City of Dunedin, Florida.

John Tornga
Vice Mayor, City Of Dunedin, Florida

Even if most people bore you, you will never be bored by Peter Kreuziger. His life experiences are indeed memorable. He spent his early years in one of the world's most beautiful monasteries. He followed his dream to live in the United States, then attended Cornell University which culminated in his establishing one of the country's finest restaurants all while having a wonderful family life. Peter constantly amazes me with his determination, resourcefulness, and passion. Two major events in the book stood out for me, the first being his educational journey with the United States Special Operations Command (SOCOM), and the second his four-month cruise around the world.

We have all learned to "read between the lines" and I implore you to do so when reading Peter's memoirs as they are very telling of who he is, and what is important to him. If you know him, his story will inspire you, and if you have not met him, you will realize this is a person that you would love to meet.

Aaron Fodiman
Publisher / Editor Tampa Bay Magazine

For the past 17 years, Peter and I have weathered many storms together, or better said, challenges, ranging from hurricane preparedness, the pandemic, a potential new store opening, just to name a few. During the pandemic, we kept on top of business developments within the city and our own properties. I never thought I would remain with the company as long as I did, but the years passed quickly and I wanted to remain a part of his successful business. While arriving with some basic food and beverage background, what I learned from him over the years was invaluable, and has brought me to the place I am today.

The highlight of these years was being awarded Employee of the Year at Bon Appétit Restaurant with two trips to Austria and Germany to further my learning experiences.

Peter opened many doors for me which, thanks to him, I can now capitalize on going forward.

Being one of Dunedin's city stakeholders, Peter again opened the doors for my continued city and civic involvement. He has shared much of the contents with me, all of which he should be proud.

Nancy Ellen Hale
Director of Public Relations, Bon Appétit, Dunedin, Florida

AUTHOR'S NOTE

To write this book, I drew upon my vivid memories along with journals, photos, and other written documentation at my disposal. I did not include last names for everyone, to protect their identity. I also left some people out of my recollections because their omission had no bearing on the validity of the event or its accuracy.

To the best of my ability, this book is a true account of my life experiences as I remember them.

INTRODUCTION

To understand why I spent my life in the hospitality business and how it came to appeal to me, I go back to a moment in my childhood that burns bright in my memory. My mother had to send me to boarding school at a very young age and because of that, she may have felt a bit guilty. She ran her own business, and my father had his own business too. Boarding school was the best option given the circumstances. Whenever I came home to visit, she tried to make things special and often took me to some really nice restaurants. The food at the boarding school left much to be desired, so these dinners were a great treat.

When I was six years old, I can still remember my mother taking me to a particularly impressive restaurant in Vienna called Wiener Rathauskeller. While sitting at our table, I noticed an older boy standing in the corner. He was wearing a stiffly starched, snow-white jacket, perfectly pressed black pants, and a white bow tie. He was maybe 13 or 14 years old and was very small for his age. I kept looking at him while I was eating my excellent dinner and I recall thinking, "I can do that, stand in the corner nicely dressed. A restaurant has great food, and they feed you. I can work here and learn the business." That's when I decided I wanted to go into the hospitality business although I wasn't able to clearly define what that meant at my young age. As I got older, I came to find the hotel business very exciting. I figured that I could get a hotel position and see the world, especially when housing and food were a part of the deal.

Over time, I set a course to make this my life work. I have been very fortunate to have achieved my goals. Throughout my career, I have met some incredibly high-performing professionals from all over the globe. I have learned that everyone has their own special strengths. I don't care how many millions of dollars someone has, what they do for a living or where they come from; if they want an extra glass of wine, I want to get it for them. I'm very happy with the career I have chosen and feel lucky that I have known since I was a boy what I wanted to do.

Working in hotels gave me more than great food. For years, I lived in luxury hotels, million-dollar condos, and had all of my needs met. Moreover, I knew I wanted to see the world. If you are a doctor or a lawyer, you have to be in one place to serve your patients or your clients. But, in the hotel business, you can go anywhere in the world.

And I did!

But like all travelers, there comes a time to find home. For nearly the last 50 years, though I have still traveled extensively, I have been able to call Dunedin, Florida my home. My wife, Mary, and I have raised our girls here. I have created successful businesses here, and have helped the town we love grow into the amazing place it is today. I've enjoyed every minute of my amazing life, the opportunities my adopted country has afforded me, and the many blessings I have been privileged to receive. This is my life story, as best as I can remember the details. I hope you enjoy reading about my adventures as much as I have enjoyed putting these memories to paper.

My Fernweh Becomes a Reality

"If you want to grow, you must
step out beyond your local boundaries
whether that is to relocate or to travel."
—YouTube

16

CHAPTER 1

THE EARLY YEARS

My mother, Dolly, was an orphan, born out of wedlock, a result of a forbidden affair in the Hapsburg aristocracy. Her birth mother was forced to give her up because of the embarrassment it would have caused the aristocratic family she was connected to. That is why my mother was sent to Hungary soon after her birth. She was very well taken care of by a well-positioned Hungarian family. But then, when the First World War broke out, non-Hungarians had to leave the country. Though Austria and Hungary used to be connected, they did not speak the same language. So, my mother was sent back to Vienna, Austria and was adopted by a working family. Her foster mother stayed at home, and her foster father worked for a furniture moving com pany. In her teens, my mother went to work for a large factory that manufactured wool into skeins.

When she was about 16 years old, she began working at one of those machines producing the skeins. She had long blonde hair, and at one point, her hair got caught in the machine and ripped half of her hair off of her head. She ultimately recovered but decided to change jobs. During the World War II, she acquired the

Above photo: Me, at about 5 or 6 months old.

lease to a store in the 5th district of Vienna which predominantly sold wool and findings for ladies' fashions. She managed this store with moderate success, but then discovered a niche. Women could come to the shop and choose from an array of colors and types of wool. Most of her customers didn't want to knit themselves, so she offered them a full-service business where they would pick the color, style, and design of their sweaters, then take their measurements and hire knitters to create their sweaters.

My mother slowly built up her business, starting with one female employee who was with us for many years. When my mother wasn't in the shop, this woman was also my babysitter.

My parents met and were married a few years before I was born in July 1943. I was born at home because my mother was afraid that since the hospitals in Vienna were overflowing with wounded soldiers and people from the war, that there was a good chance they could mix-up babies. People might never know if it was their child that was brought to their bed.

At that time, Hitler provided a list of available baby names that were publicized in the newspapers. After the child was born, if it was a boy, they got a flyer listing acceptable names for boys, and if it was a girl, they got a list of approved names for girls. Once you were born and the back of your birth certificate was completed, they would cross your name off the list if enough Peters were born, as in my case. The list was rotated over the years throughout the war. So, that's how I came to be named, Peter Werner Kreuziger.

My parents got a divorce when I was about four years old. My father subsequently moved to Baden bei Wien, a city about 25 kilometers outside of Vienna. It's a very nice little spa resort area, often visited by many tourists, mostly from Russia. There, he married his second wife, Anna, who already had three children from three different men, not husbands. She owned a shoe store that did a good business as there were lots of Russians in the area and they bought a lot of rubber boots.

There was no such thing as paid babysitters back then. So, when I was five years old, my mother sent me to a grammar boarding school in Grinzing, about 10 kilometers from Vienna. She eventually got remarried to a Polish prince by the name of Heyrowsky. He hated children so I remained in boarding schools, moving from Grinzing to Melk Abbey when I was 10. I stayed there until I was 18 years old. My mother took me out of Melk just prior to my graduation since she did not want me to become a monk. I guess she wanted the possibility of grandchildren.

Though my mother's business did okay, it was after the war, so none of us had anything. We played with stones and chestnuts that fell off the tree. There were no toys, no sports, nothing other than what you could make up yourself. I really don't remember much of my younger years; I think I have blocked it out. What I do remember of my grammar school is that we had a playground. It was next to the road, where there was a fence that you couldn't see over, but you could see through it, between the gaps in the wooden slats. I remember that when a car drove by, I would write down the license plate number of the car, just to keep myself occupied. To this day, I still look at license plates to see where people are from.

After my mother's divorce from her second husband, she had to work even harder to keep me in boarding school. I wasn't a very good student because I was too distracted thinking about my future. In contrast, what little time I spent with my father was always fun. He worked in a casino, was very good-looking and attracted the attention of beautifully dressed women. I wasn't sure these things were right but I liked the attention from his lady friends, and the candy.

Unfortunately, when my father became ill, his second wife, Anna, divorced him. Because she had treated him so poorly, she couldn't show her face around Baden bei Wien any longer. My father was really well known in the town and had lots of friends that no longer respected her. So Anna moved to Salzburg, opened another shoe store, and eventually met another man with whom she had a fourth child. My father, on the other hand, never remarried or had other children, making me an only child.

I don't really blame Anna for not taking care of my father. She already had a heavy responsibility to take care of her three children after the war. Back then, my father worked as a "croupier" in a Vienna casino. In America, this means that he made sure that bets and payouts were conducted according to casino rules. He often told me of stories where people lost everything, including one of our neighbors who was quite wealthy but who lost everything... his home, his car, and all of his possessions in one night. He told me many times that if I remembered anything he taught me, to make sure not to become a gambler. To this day, I have never gambled a single coin though I have spent many hours in many casinos around the world.

During the summers that I spent with my dad, I got to know Anna's two daughters, Ruth and Uschi. Occasionally, I would visit them along with her son, Fritz, who left home when he was 16. Nobody knew where Fritz went because he didn't tell his mother or any other family members. We later learned that he went on to Hamburg and was hired onto a ship or a freighter. For many years, nobody knew whether he was dead or alive.

The oldest daughter, Ruth, married an Italian who was a Vice President with American Express. They lived on Lake Como in Italy with their two children. The younger daughter, Uschi, also married an Italian man and lived in Italy. After Fritz finally came back, he went to the university in Austria and became an engineer. They all lived far away from their mother, realizing as adults what she was.

Many years later, I also met her youngest son, Alexander, in Salzburg. He actually turned out to be really nice guy and good looking too. He was in the Austrian military, in the guard, where you must be a certain height to even qualify. He is incredibly creative and eventually married, Isabella, a princess from Bassano, Italy. But I don't want to brag.

CHAPTER 2

MELK ABBEY

My early childhood years before attending the monastery in Austria weren't easy. And life at Melk Abbey wasn't easy either, but as an adult, I became grateful that I experienced what I did. It was such a motivator. I didn't have the luxury to fail. Even at a young age, I was happy to be on my own at the monastery.

We were 500 boys living in one building of the monastery. We all ate in one dining room that had dedicated servers by area. Partly as a sign of the times after WWII, food was still scarce, but our monks truly believed in the benefits of an empty stomach. We were often told that "a full stomach does not like to study." My mother had paid handsomely for my boarding and education at Melk Abbey yet we were living like paupers in an environment of opulence.

Another building near to where I lived were 200 additional students that had decided (or their parents had decided for them) to become priests. There was the Klausur (Cloister), where eight boys at the age of 10 had decided, or again presumably at their parent's insistence, that they wanted to become monks. These eight boys

Above photo: Melk Abbey on the Danube River, Austria.

lived like princes. Somehow, their full stomachs liked education. Of course, not all 200 seminary students went onto become priests nor did the eight students necessarily become monks.

As for the 500 of us, for breakfast we were given coffee and bread and for lunch we received soup with potatoes and vegetables, but rarely meat. For dinner, our meal wasn't much different, sort of a goulash, except for Sundays when we were treated to a canned sliced ham encased in schmaltz, a kind of animal fat which was used to keep it fresh, as there was no refrigeration at that time. That was the only way to keep it from spoiling since this ham came from America. We were allowed second helpings of every meal but it never seemed to be enough to keep our bellies full. The monks claimed that staying hungry kept our minds sharp.

From an early age, I volunteered to serve the monks their dinner meals. Between the kitchen and the monks' dining room, there was a long corridor separated by two sets of electric double doors. Coming out of the kitchen with a tray of filled plates, I could eat a whole filet of trout, or whatever happened to be on the dish, as I walked down the hall before the second set of doors would open to the dining room. I got away with it every time and did so most days that I served. I was hungry every day during those years. To explain the missing food, I simply said that it had slipped off the plate and had to be thrown away. I was a pleasant and accommodating young man, so the monks never questioned my honesty. They also found me to be cheerful, but of course I was, I was no longer hungry when I served them.

While I was at Melk, the former late Abbot Burkhard Ellegast was one of the monks. He had attended the monastery like I did and then went onto the University in Vienna, similar to seminary school, to become a priest. That took a number of years before he was ordained as a priest and came back to Melk. Just after being ordained, at probably 22 years old, Pater Burkhard moved into the Abbey and has lived there ever since. I was about 10 years old when I met him and served as his altar boy.

Pater Burkhard was my mentor as well as one of my teachers, as we had several religious and lay teachers for different subjects. Many of the boys, unlike myself, came from Melk or nearby towns, so they were strongly influenced by their parents and Melk Abbey.

As we got older, we were allowed an hour of free time on Wednesdays. Pater Burkhard's mother lived nearby in a one-room studio apartment in town. Because I was her son's altar boy at every morning's mass, I was invited to her home every Wednesday for coffee and cookies. Her invitation was to show her appreciation of my serving for her son. She would present a tray with the coffee, cream, and sugar and a plate of several cookies. She would offer me a cookie, and I would take just one, even though I was starving. Then she would ask me if I wanted more coffee. I always replied, "Yes, please," at which point she would turn around to leave for the kitchen. That's when I grabbed a handful of cookies and went into the bathroom to quickly eat them all. Of course, she noticed and filled the plate again. It was our little game.

The truth is, when the other students went into town and visited coffee houses and pastry shops, they were stealing. They didn't have money and like me, were always hungry. When I was serving Mass for Pater Burkhard, I would arrive early just so I could privately eat any food I received in a package from home. There were times in the sacristy, while getting dressed for Mass, that I would open a can of sardines and eat them all, including the oil, and then wash them down with a handful of unconsecrated hosts. I knew it was wrong. As a Catholic, we weren't (and still aren't) allowed to eat at least one hour before receiving the Body of Christ. But we all did it; we were hungry. Coming out of Melk at nearly 18 years old, I was almost as tall as I am today, and probably weighed around 140 pounds.

In addition to our studies, we were able to play sports. I played soccer against other Benedictine monasteries, and I recall one home game where I was fouled and fell. My knees were all bloody since I was wearing shorts. Our coach was of course a monk. I limped to the sideline, and he said to me, "Thank the good Lord that you had shorts on because if you had long pants, I would have to *STITCH* them!" It was okay that I had a hole in my knee and not in my pants. That's what we used to refer to as "MONKey Wisdom."

Another time I was feeling sluggish. One of the monks noticed and asked me, "What's wrong with you?"

I responded, "I'm tired".

He quickly replied, "That's not possible. You're too young to be tired." Another fine example of MONKey wisdom.

While at Melk, we also had the opportunity to act in plays that I believe we performed every February. We usually did operettas that were popular at the time, like "*Der fidele Bauer*" (*The Merry Farmer*). I usually played some part that didn't require singing because I cannot sing. Since there were no girls, some of us had to play the female parts, and I was often cast as one of them. Let me be clear though, any student that raised their hand was usually given a part to play. Rehearsals were held two or three times a week for several months before opening. The best perk of performing was that we got cookies at rehearsals on those afternoons and evenings. Did I mention that we were always hungry? These were nice plays, well attended by people from nearby towns in addition to the Melk students. They were held usually in the afternoon during "tea time" or after dinner.

A caste system was very much in place at Melk, kind of like prison, where you need protection. A classmate of mine, Martin Tauber, was a very nice young man but was intimidated by others and wouldn't stand up for himself. So, I protected him, and in return he would shine my shoes, do my laundry, and other such niceties. We looked after each other.

The student body consisted of boys from Melk and the surrounding areas but we had a lot of Viennese too. Many of the politicians and chancellors in Austria studied at Melk because of the wonderful education. Very few students stayed to actually become priests or monks but enough finished those studies to keep it going. According to their current website, the Abbey school now has over 900 students in attendance.

Most days of my schooling at Melk were the same, day after day. But once a month, we were treated to black and white Austrian or German films. I recall seeing a movie titled, *Muss Ich Denn Zum Städtele Hinaus*, a romance movie that ended with a train going out into the world. For some reason, that movie made me think about seeing the boy working in the restaurant when I was six. Maybe I could not only work in a restaurant and be well fed, but maybe I could hop on a train and see the world. Oh, there's another way to escape.

With little time left before finishing school, I knew I did not want to go back home to Vienna, a place of unpleasant memories. I had been on my own for most of my life, and I was doing just fine. I just did not yet know how I was going to accomplish my escape, but I had a bad case of "fernweh." In English, this translates to "a pain to see far-flung places beyond our doorstep. One simply wishes to be far away." I had to find a way to get out.

26

HOTEL APPRENTICESHIP

After leaving Melk Abbey, I went to Vienna for my last year of schooling. I visited with a guidance counselor who gave me a test to determine what career I would be best suited for. My results stated that I should enter the military where there was a lot of structure, law enforcement or guidance counseling. None of those professions appealed to me. Since I was a small boy, and ever since that moment in the restaurant in Vienna, I knew what kind of work I wanted to do. And now I realized the best way to travel, eat well, and live in great places was to be in the hotel business.

I applied for my first apprenticeship at the Panhans Hotel in the resort area of Semmering, two hours away from Vienna. I was there for the winter season and was instructed to do whatever was needed; we were basically slaves. My most memorable experience there was that the hotel had tennis courts that they converted to a skating rink. I served lunch and tea on ice skates. After that one season, my mother encouraged me to continue my apprenticeship in different hotels with less seasonality.

Above photo: Serving during Carnival season at the Park Hotel Mirabel.

I found a new opportunity in Hotel Europa in Innsbruck, the capital of the state of Tirol, about eight hours away from Vienna by train. It was the off season when I started, so it wasn't very busy.

I vividly recall serving three bankers who ordered red wine at lunch one day. Thankfully, they were the only occupied table as it was my first time uncorking a wine bottle, and I was very nervous. I used some force to properly turn the corkscrew, but the cork was dry so it got pushed into the bottle, and the wine splashed all over my three guests' suits as well as my white uniform. We all looked like we had just come from a bullfight! I thought for sure I was going to be fired. Instead, they were real gentlemen and handled it without much fuss. Lesson learned: make sure wine is properly stored on its side or at a slant, to ensure the cork is moist for proper bottle openings.

After the spring season at Hotel Europa, I was transferred to the newly opened Hotel Tirol, which I considered a privilege. It was directly across the street from the Hotel Europa, which was a great convenience as I only had a bicycle to get around.

As an aside, cars were scarce and costly in the early 1960s, so everyone used a bike to get around. If I decided to go dancing one night at the Schindler club, I had to ride my bike to get there. At the end of the evening, I picked up any bike outside to get home. This was a common practice in those days, and sometimes I found my own bike!

The new hotel was completely made of glass and provided beautiful vistas of the Alpine range known as "Frau Hit" or the Sleeping Lady. This hotel was highly seasonal and hosted predominantly American guests. My time there was fairly short as they closed during the winter and I wanted to complete my apprenticeship in Salzburg.

My three-year apprenticeship ended at the Park Hotel Mirabel in Salzburg, Austria and changed the course of my life. There was only one opening in the guest contact program available. I had to apply for this paid internship and was interviewed several times to earn the one spot. My new friend, Gerhardt, was already an apprentice there. To be in guest contact, I had classes one day a week in back of the house operations, like cooking and food preparation in the kitchen. If one wanted to be a cook, they had to take classes in the front-of-the-house operations and vice versa. They would cook five days a week and train in the front-of-the-house duties on the sixth day. Everyone was cross-trained, but the majority of training was on-the-job in your chosen field.

I was primarily interested in guest contact so I did not enjoy my time in the kitchen. While it could be interesting, it was not for me. I wanted to be with people and be of service to them, rather than stirring a pot of soup. Since I was a little older than the typical apprentice, I was given more responsibility, and I really liked that. It was never boring for me. It was about delivering the finer things in life. Most people do the minimum to get by but I was willing, able, and capable of doing more. I was fortunate because my managers always gave me as much as I wanted to do. I volunteered for a lot of things because I enjoyed what I was doing, and I got to meet so many nice people every day. It did not seem like work to me.

My primary training was as a server and bartender for all meals of the day and in different locations. We were exposed to room service and all the intricacies and experiences that one encounters when you go into guest rooms day and night. I have lots of stories, but none that would be appropriate to share.

The Park Hotel Mirabel was at the center of every major festival, concert, opera, and other social events that exposed me to the lifestyles of the rich and famous. It was a five-star hotel with approximately 150 rooms, a wellness center, and a "Congress Haus," a convention facility, which was physically attached where we could easily host up to 1200 guests.

Because of its elegance, size, and the beautiful, world-famous Mirabel Gardens, the Congress Haus annually hosted major events like Fasching, a season of festivities beginning on January 6th and ending on Ash Wednesday, which of course, marks the beginning of Lent, a holy Catholic season ending with Easter. The most popular of festivities were the galas held every weekend and sometimes during the week. These galas were organized by every trade and professional group as well as other organizations. Depending upon the group, some guests wore traditional regional party wear while others wore formal gowns for women and tuxedos for men. There was dancing with large orchestras from the early evening into the wee hours of the morning.

Gerhardt and I would handle all the events held in the Park Hotel Mirabel's Congress Haus. However, the hotel had to hire students from two of the nearby Hotel Schools to serve the guests drinks at bars set up throughout the convention center. Meanwhile, my colleague and I served all the snacks and sundry items. We carried trays with ten plates that held warm dishes like sausages with rolls and rolled ham that had to be sold fast before they became cold so that guests wouldn't complain. In between trays of food, I wore a "bauchladen," a basket with handles and a strap over my neck that held a variety of items like packaged nuts, salty pretzel sticks, candy, cigarettes, cigars, and even condoms. After all, attendees were there to have fun.

During these major events, we worked seven days a week. In addition to the evening events, we still had to take care of the hotel guests at the wellness center that offered massages, saunas, and steam baths. The swimming pool had to be attended to as well, with a clean poolside area and fresh towels.

The largest and most famous event that attracted people from all over the world was the Salzburg Music Festival which started on July 25th and lasted for the following six weeks. At that time, Salzburg had approximately 150,000 residents, but during the summer time, the city overflowed with international visitors. Every hotel was booked a year in advance and with mostly repeat guests. Those repeat guests that wanted to attend concerts as well knew they had to purchase their tickets in advance when arranging for their hotel stay. Sold out concerts, operas, and other events were held nightly all over the city. The first-time visitors, however, were not aware that they might not be able to get tickets to any of the concerts.

The most influential person in my apprenticeship was Herr Joseph. He was a well-known and respected concierge, an ambassador for the hotel, that I admired greatly. Any free time I had, I spent with him at the front desk of the Park Hotel Mirabel. When guests arrived through the front door, we attempted to greet them in their native language. It was easy to identify American guests that mostly came from the two coasts. The New Yorkers typically wore Brooks Brothers suits with a buttoned-down shirt and club tie. They were very serious with their attire and demeanor. Meanwhile, the Californians came in with a big smile on their face, a deep tan, an open shirt, and were so happy to be there. Though we had Russians, Germans, Italians, and other Europeans, our guests were predominantly from America. Even though we were a five-star hotel, Americans could vacation affordably in Austria at that time because of the exchange rate. One American dollar equaled 25 Austrian shillings, so life was good for them.

I admired Herr Joseph for his many skills, and I learned a lot from him. In addition to his position at the hotel, what made him so special was that he was, at the same time, a natural entrepreneur who anticipated the needs of our guests. For new guests, he always had tickets that they wanted to even sold-out events. I later learned that he purchased all of the tickets a year in advance and in bulk quantities for the best seats. When guests asked him for tickets to whichever event, he always seemed to have what they wanted, at slightly exaggerated prices. He also was able to supply other concierges from all of the other hotels, even on short notice. This was a big deal because there were several performances on any given day that he was always able to fulfill. At the end of every season, Herr Joseph ceremoniously dropped all the leftover tickets into the Salzacha River... probably in the middle of the night.

I am a product of Herr Joseph's mentorship. Remember, I had left the monastery only three years earlier, after contemplating becoming a monk. Now, I considered becoming a concierge. I never saw him handle a single situation, no matter how unreasonable or crazy the request, with anything but intelligence, wit, and a polished manner. He exuded trust, wisdom, and was always perfectly coiffed. Guests were always greeted with a smile and with total confidence that he would deliver. Regardless of a guest's sense of urgency, he never became flustered and always managed to come up with just the right tickets, at even higher exaggerated prices. Guests never seemed to mind the cost; they were just so grateful. Herr Joseph was an institution unto himself. He was known throughout Salzburg as a kind, gentle, and competent professional. I hope that I have made him proud.

After the Fasching in 1964, 20th Century Fox of Hollywood moved their entire crew and cast into our hotel for eight months to film *The Sound of Music* in Salzburg. This included the child actors, their parents, teachers, and babysitters. Julie Andrews and Christopher Plummer, however, stayed in a nearby hotel for privacy. It was truly a wonderful experience to meet and get to know all of these people on a personal basis. I saw them every day for breakfast and then again for dinner if the weather permitted. But sometimes, for two to three weeks, the weather did not cooperate, so the cast made themselves at home in the hotel, and we had a lot of fun. In fact, they insisted that I be in the movie as well and was cast as an extra towards the end of the film. This was my last time as a "movie star." There are lots of movies filmed in Austria, and I had been an extra in a few of them, but this was my favorite. These people were performers, so they brought a different life to Salzburg that I thought was very glamorous. They made me wonder how life in America would be compared to that in Europe.

We became like one big family, the hotel staff and the people from Hollywood. They knew my apprenticeship was coming to an end and asked me about what I planned to do next. I responded that, like most people in my position, I planned to go to England because I needed to learn English, as I only spoke "hotel" English, knowing just enough to understand their orders. At Melk, I had only studied Latin and ancient Greek, not too helpful in hospitality. Once I mastered English, I told them, I then planned to travel to France, Italy or some other European country to learn other languages and cultures. This practice of students going out into the world was suggested by the mayor of Vienna who spoke to the graduating class of this program back in 1895. One of the students, after his time abroad, wrote a book, *Im frack um die Welt*, about the three-year apprenticeship program instituted in Austria.

However, these actors suggested, "Come to America, we speak English. It's beautiful, it's wide open, everything is great!" In my experiences thus far, Americans had represented the United States well, from the most junior enlisted soldier to famous actors like Christopher Plummer and Julie Andrews. They had such an aura about them and were full of life, healthy, good looking, and well-kept, that I really wanted to be with them. Of course in my naiveté, I assumed everyone in America was that way.

They finished filming in October of 1964, and I completed my apprenticeship that same month. What the Americans told me had made sense. So, I went to the American Embassy in Vienna to get information on how to travel to America. They asked me what kind of visa I wanted and I replied, "What kind of visas are available?" They explained to me that they offered multiple types of visas, but I told them my intention was to only stay a year and then return to Europe. They responded that I should purchase an immigration visa, which would allow me an unlimited stay because America needed more workers with certain trades and talents. I took their advice and so that's the one I bought.

I decided to enter through New York because it was the closest. Pan American did not have direct flights from Salzburg, they had to stop in Iceland to refuel, so I decided not to fly. With money that I had saved from my $5.00 monthly salary, plus tips, (I volunteered for every event held and did quite well), I booked my passage. I chose the *SS France,* on their Cordon Bleu ocean liners, offering the fastest ocean crossing at the time of four and a half days.

Looking back now, I made the right choice. I have lived in America for nearly 60 years and am so glad I didn't go back.

CHAPTER 4
COMING TO AMERICA

I arrived in New York on December 8, 1964. After we passed the Statue of Liberty and docked at the harbor, I looked down from the bow and saw newspapers, cups, and dirt blowing in the wind. I thought to myself, "Who's idea was it to come to America?" I had left Austria with sufficient funds but arrived in New York with very little left in my pocket. I had a good time on the cruise ship. If I had the money at that time, I would never have gotten off the ship and would have gone back to Austria. But I had no choice.

I was fortunate to have someone waiting for me. Ilonka, a distant friend of my mother's who had owned a ladies' fashion shop in Vienna, was there to meet me. She had a very small one-bedroom apartment in Queens for herself and her brother. It was right by an elevated train that went by every seven minutes and rattled everything in the apartment. It was so loud, I couldn't take it, so after a few days, I looked for a job and my own place.

My biggest challenge in finding work was that I spoke so little English. The other hurdle was that in 1964, the hospitality industry

Above photo: My first car, a 1956 pink Fleetwood Cadillac.

in New York was totally unionized. I thought that my having had an excellent background and training during my three-year apprenticeship, it would be easy to find a job. I went to all the well-known hotels in New York like The Plaza, the Waldorf Astoria, The Sherry-Netherland, The Pierre, and so on. And everyone told me the same story, that they would love to have me but I needed to be a part of the union. I asked, "How do I do that?" The response was always the same; I needed to get a job and become a paying union member.

So, in the meantime, I did all kinds of jobs. In a German newspaper in Manhattan, I saw that Restaurant Associates was looking for a supervisor for the night cleaning crew at the La Guardia airport. Despite knowing hardly any English, I got the job.

On my first day, after the last flight landed at 11:00 pm, about 13 men showed up. I identified my crew because they were all carrying a broom. The first day or two went okay but by the third day, they signaled that they were hungry. They knew I had the keys to all the kitchens and storerooms, and they wouldn't start working until I fed them. What else could I do? So, I visited the storeroom for all the La Guardia concessions, pulled food out and cooked it for my crew. The kitchens were stocked by Restaurant Associates that had, I believe, 12 other restaurants around Manhattan. I worked for them as well, to replace servers on their day off, in restaurants like the Four Seasons, the Rainbow Room in the Tower Suite, Tavern on the Green in Central Park, and Zoom Zoom, a restaurant in the Pan Am building, and several others. This didn't last long, maybe a couple of weeks, until they discovered what I was doing. And then we parted friends.

My next job was as an elevator operator in the Time-Life building in Manhattan. I applied for a waiter position with the general manager of the Rainbow Room (on the 65th floor) and Tower Suite (on the 48th floor) who was a Swiss guy that spoke German. He told me they didn't have any openings but that I should take the elevator operator position until after the Christmas holidays, so I did.

One day, during the week between Christmas and New Year's Day, a man entered the elevator with a lovely, young woman on his arm to be taken to the Rainbow Room restaurant. Police officers would not allow anyone else to enter with them. It was just us three in the elevator. Once I pushed the button to the 65th floor, the man took off his right glove and extended his hand to shake mine, and said, "Merry Christmas." I later learned that the man was Harry Truman with his daughter. When I was told this, my response was, "And who is Harry Truman?" I had no idea he was a former President of the United States.

That job didn't last long either. Shortly after New Year's, now 1965, I applied once again at the Rainbow Room and the general manager said, "No, it's too slow right now." I went back to the German newspaper, and found an ad to make $154.18 a week selling magazines. I called the number and made arrangements to meet a man, John, in Times Square at 5 pm. He pulled up in a gray Peugeot, I got in next to him, and we started driving up the Hudson Highway during rush hour traffic to the George Washington bridge into New Jersey.

As we traveled further away, I started to wonder if I had made the right decision to get in his car. We were now driving on a dark road in the New Jersey countryside when he suddenly stopped the car on the side of the road.

"That's the end," I thought, "I'm dead."

But instead, a young blonde girl got into the back seat. He said, "Peter, meet Christina. She speaks German." So I took this opportunity to ask her where we were and what were we doing. She replied that we were all working for John. He drove a little further, stopped again, and then Julius (from France) got in the car. We were all about the same age, in our early 20's, all fresh new immigrants from Europe who spoke little English. Local Readers Services hired non-English speaking people to sell magazines or renew magazine subscriptions.

John also managed a hotel in Oakland, New Jersey with 10-14 rooms where we all lived. He gave us one sheet of paper that we had to memorize and taught us step-by-step on how to approach each home. Every day, John drove us to a different township, dropped us off at a street corner at 8:00 am and picked us up at the same spot at 6:00 pm. We knocked on doors all day long. People were often confused when they saw me. They couldn't understand a word I said, and that was by design. I would place my back to the door so they didn't know who I was, possibly a friend or classmate of their child. I had a canned introduction that went something like, "Please, excuse my terrible English, I am just a short time in your country. I want to speak to you about the $%^$."

"What?" they would reply. So, then I would repeat the same statement. It was winter time and very cold, so oftentimes, they would invite me in.

In my experience, American people are so generous. They typically don't say no but instead, make excuses. And since I didn't speak the language, I didn't understand their excuses and became more persistent. That's why their business model worked so well, at least for me, it did. I sold more magazines than anybody else in the company in the first six months. If you are willing to work hard rather than just going through the motions in America, you can be successful if you want to be.

After eight months, I went back to Manhattan and worked at Butler Hall Penthouse, which was the Faculty Club of Columbia University. That's where I met Mr. Staufer, who was from a region in Germany that borders Austria. He hired me, not as a waiter, but as a manager, because I wasn't a union member yet. My English was much better after selling magazines for the last eight months. The *New York Herald* was a very popular newspaper at the time, and the food writer was Clementine Pattlefort. I believe she was a graduate of Columbia many years earlier and was at the Faculty Club nearly every day for lunch. Somehow she took a liking to me and wrote a wonderful article about me.

Now, as a manager, I was a fish out of water and not feeling very productive. So finally, Staufer recommended that I apply at Luchow's (pronounced Lou Chows), a very well-known German restaurant in New York at the time. He was formerly their general manager and told me to ask for Paul. I got the job and became Peter #8 and met a fellow Austrian, Gerd #25.

Working at Luchow's was a wonderful experience because it was a very large and busy restaurant with about 100 European apprenticed waiters and cooks. It was a very desirable place to work in New York. Eastern and western Europeans who had settled in America after WWII missed their native dishes from Europe. And that's why we were really successful. Guests that came once or twice a week asked for me personally, and so I got to know them.

During my time at Luchow's, guests kept telling me that if I wanted a career in the hospitality business, I needed to go to Cornell. And I said, "What's Cornell?" I was then told that it was a university in upstate New York that specialized in Hospitality, Hotel and Restaurant Management.

On my way to Ithaca one day, in my brand-new green VW Beetle that I had bought for $2,100, I stopped in Binghamton, New York for the night. The next morning, I called the Admissions office at Cornell University to tell them I wanted to be admitted to the school. The women on the phone said she would be happy to mail the paperwork for me to fill out. I replied, "Young lady, I just came from Vienna, Austria. Surely you're not going to send me back when I'm in Binghamton now. I would like to see somebody today." I was connected with the Assistant Dean and had an appointment to see him later that day.

I presented my background and apprenticeship to the Assistant Dean. He told me that if everything I had told him was correct, and if I could prove it with my school transcripts and references translated into English and notarized, that they would love to have me as a student. I was very appreciative but explained that it would take my mother probably six months to a year to get this all done since she owned a business in Vienna. He informed me that there was no hurry, but all that information was required.

I understood but said, "Would you be so kind as to give me a letter that says what you just told me?" He agreed and reminded me that it was pending the receipt of the information he needed to accept me in their School of Hotel Administration.

I went back to New York, back to work, and made really good money. I also enrolled at Pace University on Wall Street to take my required freshman courses. I told them that I didn't want to graduate from Pace because I had already been accepted to Cornell, showing them the acceptance letter I had received from the Assistant Dean. They were happy to take my money. I also took a summer class at Columbia. I had to pass the TOEFL test, which tested my knowledge of English as a foreign language. During that year, I was able to gather all the documents required and was ready to transfer to Cornell.

CHAPTER 5

STUDYING AT CORNELL UNIVERSITY

In the fall of 1967, I started as a sophomore at Cornell, pursuing a Bachelor of Science degree with a major in Hotel Management. During my apprenticeship in Austria, hospitality was considered more of an art, where I learned how to develop my skills to service guests. At Cornell, I learned about food chemistry and took business classes to learn how to calculate food, beverage, and labor costs, as well as business law in hotel management. I learned more about the business side of the hotel industry.

For my sophomore year, I had saved enough money for tuition and living expenses. But for my junior year, I was financially embarrassed. This was a problem, so I went to the dean and asked him if there were any opportunities to earn some money while I was a student. The dean was wonderful, he offered me a job to work in the Faculty Club. Ultimately, I was promoted to the Faculty Club Manager while I was a student. Not only was this position a big honor for me, but it also paid for my education. During my tenure there, I met several Nobel Peace Prize winners, like Dr. Carl Sagan,

Above photo: Graduation Day from Cornell University, Class of 1970.

and many others along with faculty and their guests, students and their parents.

While at Cornell, I had little social life. If I wasn't in school, I was running the Faculty Club. At that time, I believe we had about 100 students per class level in the Hotel school and I think about 10% of them were international. On average, we tended to be a little bit older than the American students who had just graduated from high school before entering Cornell. Most of us had a background with apprenticeships and prior experience working in European hotels.

In the Hotel School, every Friday, we had guest speakers from various hotel chains, i.e., chief executive officers of Hilton, Sheraton, Holiday Inn, etc. On Thursday evenings, the Dean hosted an intimate dinner for any guest speakers along with 12 to 15 faculty members. I was always asked to serve that party. Often, I was asked to display the skills I had learned in Europe, like flambéing ducks and desserts, filleting dover sole, and serving Chateaubriand tableside. We had a decadent dessert using alcohol so lots of fire and flare were involved.

The dean was somewhat bragging, showing off what Cornell students could do. As a result, I got to know a lot of people from the industry.

During my junior year, I served two executives from Hotel Corporation of America (HCA) at the Faculty Club. The next morning, they tracked me down and told me that they wanted me to come to New Orleans during my summer break before my senior year. They offered me an internship at the Royal Orleans Hotel in New Orleans, a wonderful hotel, and I accepted. I had apprenticed for three years in five-star hotels, so I felt comfortable with their clientele, their operations, and the attention to detail they required.

My future responsibilities usually involved opening new hotels. The planning took about two years to open a new hotel. Once everything was approved, building permits pulled, we would start hiring people and train them according to the company's comprehensive training manuals called *Birth of a Hotel*. It was an incredible learning experience but I worked 14 to 15 hours a day. I was more interested in the real activity, rather than sitting in an office for the next 40 years of my career. To me, it wasn't really work because I really enjoyed what I was doing. We also had hotels in Boston, Hartford, Connecticut, New York, San Francisco, New Orleans, Bermuda, and other locations.

One of my favorite Cornell professors was Professor Wanderstock. His class was on Meats, Fish, and Fowl. He received his doctorate at Cornell, from the School of Agriculture, and he took us on a field trip to a kosher slaughterhouse. It was frightful. We entered the back of the slaughterhouse where the Rabbi enters. They had a conveyor belt that goes around, that they called the Stairway to Heaven. They claim that the animals don't know what's happening, but I think they knew. You could hear the animal noises and smell their blood.

Upon entering, the first thing I saw was the back of the Rabbi's head, holding the cow's head to give him an ear-to-ear throat cut. The animal was fully alive, no tranquilizers or anesthetics. The Rabbi had a special knife, so after he cut the head off, he used his thumb and finger to examine the knife, to make sure he hadn't nicked the bone. If he had, it would automatically disqualify the cow from being kosher. It was rough to watch, but the Rabbi did what he was supposed to do.

I also spent one semester living in Professor Wanderstock's home because he rented it out to students.

I had two others classmates from Austria who I met at Cornell. I believe there were several of us from Europe. The other two guys knew each other because they both had worked on a cruise ship and had traveled together for about four or five months around the world. They also had gone through a European apprenticeship.

These two guys were like me, a little bit older and had worked as apprentices for two to three years before arriving in America.

One guy, Udo, had an Austrian mother and a German father. The other guy, Gert, had a Swedish background, but I believe his father was an Austrian surgeon. Most of us came from broken homes, largely due to the war.

I was always quizzing them on what they wanted to do after graduation. Udo told me he definitely wanted to work in hotels but, sooner or later, he wanted to get into teaching. Teaching? That was the last thing on my mind. I asked Gert the same question and he told me that he didn't care. But at some point he did care and became the Dean of Students at Harvard University.

I told them I absolutely wanted to graduate. Also, to get my visa to America, I had taken an oath to join the American military. This was during the Vietnam War and I felt an obligation to the U.S. I suggested to them both, to join me in the military. I remember saying, "Look at their beautiful green coats that the Army GIs wear, they get us into good physical shape," and so on. I almost had Gert convinced but not Udo. He wanted nothing to do with the Army.

To backtrack, while I was a student, I took classes in the Platoon Leaders Class (PLC) program for the Marine Corps because they were the only branch of service that would even talk to me since I was not yet an American citizen. The Army, Navy and Air Force would only admit American citizens into the officer's program, without exception.

As you can understand, after graduating from Cornell, I didn't want to go in as a grunt, but wanted to become an officer. Our Colonel was also the ski and soccer coach, so I had a good relationship with him. Besides, I was running the Faculty Club.

On April 18, 1969, members of the Cornell University Afro-American Society (AAS) occupied its student center, Willard Straight Hall, to protest what they believed was Cornell's institu-

tional racism, its biased judicial system, and its slow progress in establishing a Black Studies program. Gun-wielding black students seized control of a campus building in April 1969. Cornell University descended into anarchy.[1]

In 1969, the African-American students at Cornell marched to the Student Union and took it over. They would not let anybody in. And every year, the Hotel School students would host a stage performance. I participated in that as well along with an African-American friend of mine, Michael. His family owned the concession stands in the Washington Redskins football stadium. We had a skit prepared to do together in our large theater. We were not supposed to even be talking to one another during those times, but we were friends. So, I asked him, "Michael, should we go forward with this skit?" Classes had been canceled, and most students were going home though the semester hadn't finished yet. Those students had guns, and it was touch and go for a while. But then I said, "What do we have to lose? I mean, you're black, I'm white, let's get on the stage. We'll be fine."

For our skit, I borrowed a cow from the School of Veterinary Medicine. Cows have seven stomachs and for academic education, they made an opening in each stomach so students could see how food was processed through each stomach. Our chemistry professor, Mrs. Laura Lee Smith, was in her 70's, wore a white lab coat and had gray hair. As an aside, her husband invented potato chips, and also worked as a professor in the School of Agriculture. Anyway, so I put on a bathing suit, put a white coat over it, then placed a wig on my head and showered it with white powder. For my part of the skit, I walked on stage, pulling the cow. Then I would let the cow go for a bit, and then slap my wig so that the powder went everywhere, even on Michael, who was covered in white. The students were laughing hard because it was way over the top.

---

1   *Taken from article, Student Takeover at Cornell University (1969) by Steven Rosino and Alan Singer in the NJCSSJournal.*

Our two toughest courses were Inorganic and Organic Chemistry. Mrs. Smith really knew her stuff, but it was a blessing that those classes were canceled, including the final exams.

TIME magazine had an article about this event, with one of the black students carrying a rifle and wearing shot gun shells across his chest.

CHAPTER 6

AFTER GRADUATION

Prior to my graduation in 1970, I learned that the interview process in America was different from what I had known in Europe. I didn't want to work for most of the companies I had interviewed with, but I wanted the experience. I had a made a good decision to earn a degree at Cornell. The proof was in the pudding; I interviewed with 26 companies and received 25 job offers.

Approximately 50% of the graduates in my class went for advanced degrees in accounting and law. The remaining went into the hotel and restaurant industry. A good number of them had families that owned hotels and restaurants in different parts of the world. They went onto Asia, some went back to Europe, and those remaining stayed in North America.

As an example, Sonny Lin was from Hong Kong, he was extremely bright and industrious. Prior to coming to the Cornell School of Hotel Administration, he had studied at Lausean in Switzerland. His father was the importer of fruits and vegetables for Hong Kong but always wanted to be in the hotel business. Sonny interviewed

*Above photo: Playing DJ at Someplace Else in
Jacksonville, Florida.*

with many hotel companies but was not offered a position. His father told him, "Come home, and I will build a 1,000-room hotel that you will run and ultimately own." And he did.

After I graduated, a classmate of mine by the name of Peter B, who is a billionaire today, invited me to work at a new nightclub in Jacksonville, Florida. They were opening this large disco there and wanted to add a steakhouse restaurant. There were two brothers who owned Fletcher Development Corporation, which owned hotels, restaurants, golf and country clubs, housing developments, and more. Initially their father started the company as an insurance company, which they also owned. One brother lived in New York with his wife. He was a blue-jeans, cowboy boots kind of guy. I'm not sure how he was involved. The other, Jerome, worked in the real estate division. They built Baymeadows, which is a big golf and country club on the south side of Jacksonville which was nothing when we went there.

The bar was called Someplace Else, and I was hired to manage it and help establish the restaurant. It was a good deal for me because everything was paid for, my food, housing, car, even my clothes down to my dry cleaning. We had to look the part and dress sharply, of course.

Someplace Else was a real discotheque nightclub, typical of that era, built on the St. John's River, close to the Gulf Life Tower (a big high rise), and the Prudential Tower across the river in downtown. Across the highway was also the Jacksonville Memorial Hospital. It was the early 1970's, and from the moment it opened, it was a big success. Every night, we had many doctors and nurses intermingling in our club. This job didn't really align with my experience or career path, but I was intrigued. We became the largest liquor-selling operation in northern Florida. When it was really busy, we had to hire police just to keep people away.

The design of this place was incredible. We had a lighted dance floor with lights underneath that moved to the beat of the music.

The building had no windows even though we could have had the best view in town. There were three sections, designed like a Y; each one with large projection screens. One showed videos of the finer things in life, like nice clothes, jewelry, and fancy cars like Ferraris and Porsches. The other showed black and white films like Laurel and Hardy and the third one, was more sensual in nature, but not vulgar.

We had a DJ playing the popular music of that time, and the dance floor was always filled with people moving to the lights and the beat. The Men's and Women's bathrooms were way in the rear of the club on purpose, and each had a telephone. If a girl was on a date with a guy she didn't like, she could head way back to the bathroom and call Karl, another friend, and ask him to send the guy home.

When Fletcher Development Corp opened Baymeadows, I was the first resident in the complex and lived in a beautiful company furnished apartment. We hired my friend, Gerd, to run the steakhouse and he became the second resident of Baymeadows.

While I enjoyed my time in Jacksonville, after a year or so, I realized this was not really my career path. Working into the wee hours of the morning since the bar stayed open until 3 am, was not really my speed. So, I went back to New Orleans and new opportunities.

I was approached by four investors: a lawyer, a builder, an entrepreneur, and the owner of the New Orleans Saints at the time. They put up the money for a new hotel in New Orleans. I accepted the position at Le Pavillion Hotel, which was still under construction and within walking distance to the new football stadium also under construction. When I took the job, they were just beginning to hire staff.

To backtrack a little, during my summer internship at the Royal Orleans, because I spoke German, the HCA owners asked me to fill out immigration papers for two young German cooks that worked for them in Bermuda. I went back to Cornell University for my senior year and never met the people on the immigration papers. After the two cooks were approved, they were sent to the Royal Orleans. One of them was Karl, my current partner of more than 50 years.

When I returned to New Orleans to open Le Pavillion, because I knew everyone in the hotel, I asked about the two young men I had filled out immigration papers for the year prior, to see how they were doing. I learned that Karl was considered a very good cook, a hard worker, diligent, reliable, and knew his way around the kitchen. Unfortunately, the other guy was considered a clown. I met with Karl and decided he was right for the Chef position.

When I brought Karl over and introduced him as the new Chef for the hotel, they liked him but said he was just a kid. They wanted a real Chef. I replied, "Well, look, if you want to second guess me before we even start, you need somebody else. I'm not your guy." I also added, "If you don't like his performance, I will assume the responsibility. I know who he is and what he can do." They kept him.

We got Le Pavillion opened, and it was a very impressive hotel. Our grand marbled staircase had been purchased and shipped from the Grand Hotel in Paris and was a focal point of our lobby. But after the hotel opened, I again considered what I wanted to do next. I loved a challenge, and that one was completed.

As a Cornell alum, I received a weekly bulletin that listed new opportunities by position, along with contact information, the salary range, etc. on all seven continents. Since coming to America in 1964, graduating from Cornell in 1970, and having worked seven days a week for over two years thereafter, mostly in warm climates, I missed skiing. Coming from Austria, I had skied from a young age and felt I needed to get back to the snow.

I found an ad in the Cornell bulletin for a restaurant manager in Aspen, Colorado that got my attention. I contacted Dr. John Cheek who was the owner of that restaurant in addition to being the dean of the Russian language department at Vanderbilt University in Tennessee. As an aside, he was also the heir of the Maxwell House coffee dynasty. During our call, he invited me to interview in Nashville. I responded: "Sir, I would be delighted to come to Nashville to do so. I can come in my Brooks Brothers suit and tie, my shiny shoes and school pins on the lapel and make a fine Ivy League impression but I have a different idea to show you who I am and what I can do. Why don't you come to New Orleans instead and see what I have accomplished in opening Le Pavillion Hotel?" I wanted him to see all our food and beverage facilities, our restaurants, bars, banquet rooms and nightclub. Dr. Cheek replied that my suggestion made good sense. He had a private plane and flew down to meet me.

Upon his arrival to New Orleans, I was standing on top of the grand marble staircase for maximum affect. He was hooked from the start. It turned out that he was a lovely man. After taking him on a thorough tour of the hotel, I suggested another idea I wanted him to consider. Rather than hiring me as an employee that he had to supervise, I asked him to consider leasing the restaurant to me. I would pay him rent instead of him paying me a salary. Dr. Cheek thought it was a really good idea and that's what I did.

I resigned from the Le Pavillion Hotel after being there for 18 months and asked Gerd (#25), who had been a waiter at Luchow's, to come with me. When I was in Cornell, I was going back and forth during Christmas and summer vacations to earn some more money for the next semester. When I first started at Luchow's, I literally had no money, and Gerd let me stay in his home when I was in New York. We became good friends, and I never forgot how good he was to me. I convinced him into moving to Aspen and becoming the Chef.

We put everything we owned into a U-Haul and drove to Aspen. It was the end of November before we even found housing. The ski season had begun, and we were out skiing as well. Gerd was a good skier, but uncontrolled, and he managed to break his leg.

Since he could not ski anymore, he worked the restaurant every day. In the meantime, I skied every day and worked the night shift. We worked for only that one season, but I knew that once our lease was up, I would be looking for a new opportunity.

When the season finished, the town consisted of Gerd, the mailman, a dog on Main street and me. Gerd went to work for another restaurant nearby and became the manager for one of the two that were open year-round. I moved on to my next venture while Gerd stayed in Aspen for the next 30 years.

CHAPTER 7

ON THE MOVE AGAIN...
AND AGAIN

After closing the restaurant in Aspen, I again went to the Cornell bulletin and saw that Princess Hotel Corporation had an open position for a Food and Beverage Director to help open the Southampton Princess, a 600-room, 5-Star Hotel in Bermuda. One of my classmates at Cornell was the Resident Manager there, so I got the position and to Bermuda I went.

We opened 12 restaurants on the property. They had a golf course, a tennis club, night clubs, and a main dining room that seated 800 guests. It was the largest property I had ever managed to this point. We also housed somewhere around 700 employees from multiple nations. I learned that you can't put Ecuadorians and French people together; they do not get along. I was able to use my European training, learning different customs and managing their sensitivities.

After the hotel opened, we hosted some wonderful conventions in Bermuda. The Golden Circle convention brought IBM's top 100

Above photo: Working at the Southampton Princess, Bermuda.

highest producing salespeople globally, along with their spouse, to Bermuda for, I think, four or five days. Also, there were about 200 leadership and administrative team members for a total of nearly 500 people. The lowest man on the totem pole of those 100 salespeople made a commission that year that exceeded a million dollars. This was in the early 70's, so it was the best of the best in attendance. And they were treated to an amazing experience with everything paid for. They even hired a flotilla of deep-sea fishing boats brought over from the Bahamas for their use.

There was only one exception: no alcohol. The founder of IBM was not in favor of drinking and even though he had passed away, the rule still applied for all of their events. So, we set up bars in the elevators during their meals so attendees could leave the function, take a ride up to the sixth floor and come back down. They would make excuses to ride the elevators just so they could grab a drink. They had to pay for the alcohol, but everything and anything they wanted was given to them without charge. I don't think IBM does this anymore, but I managed this convention for them twice while at the Princess Southampton.

I met lots of guests in the sauna, after I played a little tennis in the afternoon. In the sauna, everybody in there is without "textiles" and an equal. One time, one guy asked another, "So, what brings you to Bermuda?"

The other guy responded, "I'm here with the Golden Circle. You know, I've been with IBM for 30 years, and I could have retired a long time ago. But my goal in life was to once be included in the Golden Circle meeting. And that is why I'm here today."

I thought, "That's amazing!"

Because the property was so large, from a professional perspective, it was difficult to retain that personal touch with employees. I stayed in Bermuda for about a year and a half, working every day until the hotel opened. Bermuda is an island, 28 miles long, and about a mile at its widest point. I learned that there is such a thing as "island fever." Sometimes it felt like a prison to me because I couldn't leave, but eventually I did.

I came to Bermuda from America, but most other employees came from Europe. When I told the office that I had island fever, that very night, they arranged for me to take a Pan Am flight to New York and gave me a room at a big, impressive hotel on 6th avenue. I was near the wonderful Carnegie Deli where they make big sandwiches of corned beef and pastrami and many traditional Jewish dishes. Famous people often enjoy meals there.

I enjoyed the break but I experienced a bit of a scare. One night, I was in bed and the room was dark. I was woken up from the sound of someone in the room to see the shadow of a man rifling through the dresser drawers. I hollered out, "Hey, what are you doing?"

Upon realizing he was caught, he ran out of my room. I immediately called the police and waited for two hours before anyone came.

When the police arrived to my room, I asked what had taken them so long. The cop's reply was, "Do you think you're the only one who got robbed in this hotel tonight?" The police had been in the hotel for two hours, going room to room where the robbers had been seen.

After my New York vacation, I went back to Bermuda but soon gave my notice to leave anyway. I read a notice in the Cornell bulletin about a job that appealed to me. I had an interview in Boston where I met Bill R. who was supposed to become my boss at a ski resort on Boyne Mountain in Michigan. This was not a mountain, more of a mole hill. I got the job and gave my six-week notice. I flew back to Boston and Bill said, "Oh, by the way were not going to Michigan, we're going to Scott's Inn in Columbus, Ohio."

The first night I checked in, I walked out into the corridor to find a cow in the hallway. The Ohio State Fair was on that week and apparently, the cows were too valuable to leave at the fair, so they were "guests" of ours. The Ohio State football team would also stay at our hotel before their games, not to compare them to the cows.

I did find a nice apartment in a very woodsy area nearby the hotel. Ohio is a very dreary state. The people are nice but it's depressing weather wise. No sun or skiing, so I only worked there for about six months.

Fortunately, Scott's Inn management also had a hotel in Orlando. The hotel rooms were ready to go but the food and beverage area, banquet rooms, and bars had yet to be set up. I was sent to Orlando since I had bought the first million-dollar kitchen for Le Pavillion. I wanted to use the same company to buy the kitchen equipment for this new hotel so I contacted them and chose what we needed at the Orlando hotel.

I called corporate and said, "Okay, we're all set, I need a check for $250,000 for the down payment."

They told me I had to wait as they still had no occupancy papers. Since there were no guests, all day long, I sat by the pool and answered the phone. One day, I got a call from a bank saying I was terminated. The bank had apparently taken over the note on the hotel.

My response to this fellow from the bank was, "Are you firing me?"

"Yes," he replied into my ear.

"Well, you can't do that?" I responded.

"Why not?" he asked.

"Because my contract isn't with you. You didn't hire me, and you can't fire me. If I don't get the pay I am owed, I will start selling furnishings in the hotel," was my answer.

Within days, they sent a check for what I was owed and I moved on to my next opportunity.

I called Bill Ratzel. He was working at the Eden Rock on Miami Beach right next to the other most famous hotel in Miami, the Fontainebleau. Howard Garfinkle had just bought and renovated the Eden Rock. Their motto was "The Rock Rolls Again." Bill was now the General Manager, and he said that they needed help running the bar called Love and the restaurant called Flowers. This was to be a temporary assignment so off to Miami I went.

I stayed in the hotel with every amenity including the sauna, and lived large. Bill also lived in the hotel, and ate the same thing every night: shrimp cocktail and a New York strip with all the fixings. This was a union hotel, mind you, and Bill did not get along with the union representative (rep). Shortly after my arrival, Bill was poisoned by way of his dinner and was out of work for a while.

I co-managed the nightclub with the union rep's sister who was good looking and a flirt. I was her protection so we became fast friends. She talked to her brother who happened to be head of the union and encouraged him to offer me the Shop Steward position at the Eden Rock, reporting to him. Fortunately, I did not speak Spanish and thought better of getting involved considering Bill's illness. I declined the offer and left after a few months, as did Bill.

CHAPTER 8

COLONY BEACH AND TENNIS RESORT, LONGBOAT KEY, FLORIDA

Now that I was back in the States, I knew I wanted to remain. I called my friend, Tom Clarkson, who I knew from my time in Bermuda. He was working at the Colony Beach and Tennis Resort on Longboat Key in Florida.

"I was thinking about you," he said. "I could use someone with your knowledge and expertise. I want to redo all the food and beverage at the Colony, new menus, fresh ideas. Would you be available?"

I told him I was, and so I headed to Florida to spend time in Longboat Key on the Gulf of Mexico.

The owner of Colony Beach was a unique individual. Dr. Murph Klauber was from Buffalo, New York, married for the third time to a tough German woman. He had a God-given talent for taste, not in food, but for clothing, cars, and all the finer things in life.

Above photo: My picture on the cover of a local magazine while working at the Colony Beach & Tennis Resort.

His wardrobe was from all over the world. He wore beautiful shoes and jackets. Murph's business partner, Joe P, had made his money by buying and building post offices and leasing them back to the Postal Service. Joe's wife was a water ski champion who performed at Cypress Gardens in Florida. When the two gentlemen bought the Colony Beach, they tore down the existing little wooden huts and created a 275-unit condo, "condominionized" resort with a heavy emphasis on tennis. It was a spectacular property. In fact, the property is currently being re-developed into a 5-star luxury resort.

As a condominium resort, the owners were permitted to spend two weeks a year complimentary, and then after that, if they stayed longer or visited more often, they had to contribute to the rental pool. The Colony received 53% of the revenue that came from room rentals and the owners got 47%. The difference was for housekeeping and maintenance of the property. Many of the buyers were from Murph's hometown in Buffalo, New York.

One day, early on, I had breakfast with Jerry Thirion, a friend of Murph's, who was serving as a goodwill ambassador at The Colony. Jerry had had a successful career selling Corvettes in Buffalo, and Murph was his best customer. There was a new server who Jerry introduced me to; Mary was a student at the Miami University in Oxford, Ohio and was working there for the summer to earn some money. Her parents had a condo in St. Armand's Towers where she was living, and Jerry lived in the same building. This particular morning, Mary brought breakfast to Jerry as usual, and I had ordered a cup of coffee. She brought my coffee with shaking hands and dropped the spoon onto the floor. I said, "You don't need to be nervous, but I actually wanted a coffee without the foot bath in the saucer." So, that was my first impression of Mary, and her first impression of me as well. It went over like a lead balloon, of course.

Mary worked there during the summertime, and I wasn't long out of college myself. I could remember that one of the things I treasured most at Cornell were the meals that I served to the dean and his guests. College students always appreciate a nice meal before going back to college food. Since she was leaving to go back to school, I invited Mary to dinner, initially at the Colony. It was such an unusually busy day, inside and outside, including a barbeque we were hosting on the beach. It was getting late for dinner, about 11:00 pm when I was finally able to leave. I still had to go back to my condo to get a shower, and it was raining heavily.

Meanwhile, Mary had been sitting at the bar drinking refreshments, waiting for me. In fact, I didn't recognize her until the bartender told me that my date had been patiently waiting for me for the last four hours. I was struck by the sight of this pretty young woman with long blonde hair falling down around her shoulders. I had never seen her hair because it had always been under a hat since the entire staff dressed in tennis attire. The name was Colony Beach and Tennis Resort and as the name implied, tennis was the main focus. At any given moment, a guest might be in need of a tennis partner and someone on the staff would be enlisted to jump in and play. So, Mary, even as a server, was always dressed in sporty attire and a cap that hid her beautiful hair.

We went to the Hilton on Longboat Key and had a memorable dinner. But, with all of her alcohol consumption, she was looking cross-eyed at me. I have to say, because she was an employee, I never let myself be attracted to her. I candidly never thought of her like that. Mary was untouchable as far as I was concerned. She was very nice and had a lot going for her. My purpose in taking her to dinner was to thank her for her summertime work.

She didn't go back to school for a few weeks and, as I said, was staying in her parents' condo in the same building as Jerry's. As friends, Mary and I would visit Jerry and his wife for dinner or watch football games. She was studying interior design and offered to help me find and purchase a bean bag chair for my apartment. I didn't make a second good impression as I forgot my wallet and she had to pay for my new chair, temporarily.

I stayed at the Colony Beach & Tennis Resort for several years until Murph ran into financial challenges. The relationship with owners changed over the years as they didn't keep up the property as originally intended. So, Mary went back to school, and I moved on to a position in Palm Harbor, Florida. After Mary graduated in 1976, she moved back to Sarasota into her parent's condo and found a job with Jacobson's on St. Armand's Circle.

I found the position at Innisbrook in Palm Harbor in the Cornell bulletin one final time. Jim Pierce had been the GM at Innisbrook and attended the Hotel School at Cornell like I did. He died in an airplane accident while on a vacation, so there was no GM when I interviewed with Bob H. Bob H. was the assistant manager, and thought he was getting the open GM position, where he would be in charge of everything regarding food, beverage, and the hotel. Bob hired me as the night manager based on my interview. The way he acted during the interview made me think, this guy will never keep this job. I was right. After a short while on the job, I was promoted to Director of Operations and Bob resigned.

I was in charge of everything except golf and tennis. By the time I left, I was the Executive Vice President of the resort. The owner and CEO, Harvey Jones, owned a Lear jet, and he put the flags of each of his executive team member's countries on the side of the plane including mine—Austria. I asked him once how he had come up with the name Innisbrook. It turned out that when he went to build the property, he remembered an alleyway that was named Innisbrook from his hometown in Ohio. He liked the sound of it so he named the whole property after an alleyway.

I brought Karl to Innisbrook to be the Head Chef thus improving our food service. At Innisbrook we worked with Fortune 500 companies who would come in to host their quarterly, semi-annual or annual meetings because we had two huge facilities next to one another. The names of those facilities have since changed but at that time, there were called Harston Hall and Tameron Hall, which was named after our sister property in Colorado. Each hall could seat over 1,000 people for meals.

Amway International would hold their convention with about 2,000 people at a time. I recall one of their conventions around the 4th of July weekend. They all came in a day or two earlier and stayed through the 4th. We held a fireworks display on the property for them. On their last evening, after their desserts, I went up on the stage to tell them that all of our employees, management and ownership were so appreciative of their visit, and that we wished them all the best in their future endeavors. I also told them that they had been the nicest people we'd had in a long time.

Afterwards, they all stood up and started chanting that they wanted to meet the Chef. So, I told them I would try. They sat down again, and I went into the kitchen. Karl had been long gone for the night, but we had a German speaking chief steward in charge of the dishwashers. I grabbed him, made him put on a Chef's coat and hat, and told him to come out with me on the stage. I told him not to speak, just take some bows. So, he did, and all 2,000 people stood up and applauded him while he took several bows as I instructed. I think he really enjoyed the adulation as he kept bowing and saying "thank you" as they applauded him.

64

Building Businesses & Lasting Relationships

"The further you go, the greater the gain."
—YouTube

CHAPTER 9

MCKOWN'S SEAGULL TO BON APPÉTIT

Dr. David O'Day was a board member at Innisbrook and an interesting individual who I became friends with during our time together there. Since he was a homeowner at the resort, he often came to my office in the late afternoon to share a cup of coffee. During one of these visits, I told him that I was thinking about leaving Innisbrook.

"Oh, you should go and visit McKown's Seagull. See if you can make a deal with the owner there. He's an unusual person," he stated. He added that it was close by without much moving involved. He said this because I had been thinking of moving to an Indian reservation in the four-state area where Innisbrook had another hotel.

So, I drove to Dunedin. The restaurant was unbelievably run down. The smell outside was awful; it was low tide, and all I saw were mud flats since the dock didn't exist at that time. I thought to myself, "Maybe I'm in the wrong place."

Above photo: Bon Appétit in the early years.

I went in, and there were maybe two or three people sitting at the bar that afternoon. The floors were covered with what were once white shag rugs that had turned dark.

The bartender asked me, "Wanna beer?" He didn't know me, and I didn't know him.

I answered that I wasn't interested, but he persisted and gave me a beer. At that time, it was rude to drink out of the bottle so he asked me if I wanted a glass.

I said, "Yes, please." He gave me the glass, setting it next to the Budweiser. I took one look at the glass and asked him, "Do you mind if I drink out of the bottle?" I took napkins and wiped the bottle before sipping.

He asked me, "So, what brings you here?"

I told him that Dr. O'Day had referred me because there was a possibility that the owner was interested in selling the business. A little background: Dr. O'Day was the president and one of the owners of Clearwater Oaks Bank. Apparently, the restaurant owner was in default of his mortgage payments for several months. Before moving down to Florida, Dr. O'Day was a corporate psychologist for IBM, so he had a lot of insight from his training.

I asked the bartender, now realizing he was the owner, if this was all of the restaurant. He said no and told me to follow him upstairs.

The beams were dark from nicotine. There was a mirrored ball hanging from the middle where dancing was supposed to happen, though I never saw it. The only events held upstairs, I learned later, were Rotary lunches. Unlike the restaurant that exists today, our smaller banquet room was then an open-air terrace with no roof and indoor/outdoor green carpeting. After showing me around, he went downstairs to the kitchen and came back with a bucket of suet, which is beef and pork fat.

He took it out to the terrace and said, "Watch this!" He picked up a piece of meat and threw it into the air, and seagulls came from everywhere. He did this on a daily basis. I guess, thus the name, McKown's Seagull. Surprisingly, there were people standing downstairs that were getting "rained on" by seagulls.

I asked him how many dinners he usually served a night. His response was maybe 12-25.

After that visit, I couldn't see myself having a restaurant at that location. I returned to Innisbrook where Karl, our Chef, asked me how it was. I said, "It's a dump. You don't even have to go there." But he still wanted to see it, so we drove down again together. Karl loved it!

He thought it was beautiful, "We can fix it!" he said. So, that's how the McKown's Seagull came to be ours.

I had never been to Dunedin before visiting McKown's Seagull. I lived and worked on the Innisbrook property and commuted to Durango, Colorado once or twice a month on the company's Lear jet. I had never heard of Dunedin, so I started driving around. Main Street didn't exist at that time, but instead, State Road 580 ended at our seawall. I walked along the street toward the restaurant and saw a few buildings, storefront windows were broken or boarded up, garbage was in the street, and tumbleweeds were literally blowing around. The train station was open with two trains passing through daily: one in the morning and one at night. Parking meters were on that road, (but there were no cars); years later it would be reconfigured into Main Street as it is today. I rarely saw cars. There was a large lot next to a warehouse owned by Sun Bank where garbage was piled up. I recall only a few businesses other than Sun Bank, one being an engineering firm. There was no one walking around because there was no reason to walk around.

Harold "Corby" Corb worked for Dr. O'Day and handled the transaction for us. Karl and I became 50/50 partners, each investing $5,000. The bank financed the remaining sales price to purchase the business and all of its assets, which did not include the building. At the closing table, the room was filled with bankers, attorneys, and accountants. I went to hand the previous owner the check when I saw a hand come from behind me that took it instead. It was the IRS. I don't know what happened after that, but I did learn that the bank was repaid as well. We did repay Clearwater Oaks Bank within a year of closing.

So, that's how we got started. After closing on the business, we didn't have much money left but we started renovating what we could afford to do. We sprayed down the beams with acid to clean off the years of nicotine. We ripped the carpet out, put new carpeting down and deep cleaned everything. When we turned the tables upside down, cockroaches came out from the legs. The chairs were small and pitiful, but we had no other choice but to open that way.

McKown did not own the building but had 33 years remaining on the lease. At that time, I thought, "33 years, that's pretty good." I was 30 years old, and in 33 years, I'd be 63 years old and could retire.

The man who did own the restaurant and parking lot was Mr. Wallace. He lived across from Edgewater Arms by himself. He had two daughters, one who lived in Dunedin and had never married. She took care of her father as he was quite elderly by then. The other had married an attorney and lived in Chicago.

Sometime after opening Bon Appétit, I visited Mr. Wallace to introduce myself. I recall him saying, "Oh, yeah, Peter, I heard you're doing a good job."

I began, "I want to talk to you about buying your property." He replied, "My property is not for sale."

He continued by saying, "I gave everything already to my daughters, and they are in charge. I paid so much in taxes in my life, I don't want to pay any more. I'm very happy."

I repeated, "You are very happy? Then I want to make you twice as happy. I'll give you $2,000 a month. In return, you double the remaining time on the lease of 33 years to 66 years."

Quickly, he replied, "You got a deal!" And that is how we remained for 47 years in the same place.

In the early years of Bon Appétit, I felt it could use a lot more business. There was a Bert Powers Oldsmobile dealership on SR 580. Their sales manager would come to Bon Appétit for lunch two to three times a week.

One day, I approached him and said, "Listen, there is such a thing as a free lunch if you work with me. Bring your excess used car inventory down to our parking lot, and your lunch is free any day of the week."

He thought it was a great idea, and for a long while, our parking lot, which had been mostly empty, was now over 50% filled with used cars.

Afterwards, I saw some of our competitors, like the owners of Pappas in Tarpon Springs, Siple's in Clearwater, Aaron Fodiman from the Kapok Tree in nearby Safety Harbor drive by and see our nearly full lot. Of course, if they had come in, they would have seen no one inside.

A little about fine dining

When I left Europe in 1964, I was totally tuned into the European way and thought we were light years ahead of America when it came to fine dining. In New York City, a special dinner usually started with onion soup, then a salad with a choice of Russian dressing, Roquefort or oil and vinegar. The entree would be either a filet mignon or sirloin steak and a baked potato with sour cream, chives, cheese, and bacon bits. For dessert, it was apple pie, and if you were really going big, with a slice of cheddar over the warm pie served with ice cream.

But when Europeans like myself came over with professional apprenticeships who had their education in European hotel schools, many opened restaurants in the U.S. They introduced how to de-bone a duck, filet a fish, or make cherries jubilee or bananas foster in front of guests. And then the French made a big entree into America. They were probably the leaders of all European nations in classical cuisine, from Chef Augusto Escoffier who started in London at the first Ritz. He was a highly trained French chef and wrote many books. Slowly, people started to venture out to restaurants offering different cuisines. Most Americans had not been exposed to different cuisines.

Now I feel Americans are light years ahead of Europeans. Austrian and German food is very good, but rather limited. European restaurants don't have the variety of choices; they have pork but very little beef. In Austria, they have milk cows meaning the beef is tough so the best way to eat beef is when it's boiled. In my opinion, America is number one in the world in beef production; it tastes good and is easy to eat because the animal is different in the U.S. than in Europe.

The French are masters of sauces. There is an individual that works as the garde-manger, the French word, who works only with cold foods like appetizers, cold sauces, and accompaniments like raspberry sauce, coulis, that goes over ice cream and other dishes. Then there is an individual that cooks nothing but vegetables; he is the entremetier. The person that cooks only fish is the poissonnier while the boucher grills and prepares all the steaks, lamb, pork, etc. Then, there is also the Chef pâtissier for desserts. A typical stove has four sides and heating plates. So, as orders come up, the entremetier puts the ordered vegetables on the plate, then hands it to the boucher or poissonnier who places the correct protein on the plate and hands it off to the garde-manger to place whatever else was ordered. The entire process is somewhat like an assembly line.

The Head Chef makes sure to taste everything before the service starts to ensure the food is properly seasoned, is the right consistency, and the right color because we eat with our eyes too. They are more or less also expediters to ensure the flow from the kitchen to the server is efficient who then make a final inspection of every plate before it is served to guests.

The menu at Bon Appétit has changed many times over the years, mostly due to consumer tastes. True fine dining requires education, with servers having been through apprenticeships. It is more expensive to run, and few businesses survive. There are no more than five restaurants in the Tampa Bay area that have been in business for nearly 50 years like Bon Appétit.

CHAPTER 10

RECONNECTING WITH MARY

I had stayed in touch with Jerry Thirion over the years and called him to invite him to my new restaurant, Bon Appétit, in Dunedin. I gave him the address and while on the call, I asked him what ever happened to Mary Miller. He replied that she was in Sarasota working on St. Armand's Circle. I suggested that he bring her along.

Bon Appétit opened on October 17, 1976, and we had been open only a week or two when Jerry brought Mary with him to dine as my guests. It was a long drive for them, they got lost a couple of times and Mary kept asking Jerry where they were going. Once they crossed the Skyway Bridge, she asked Jerry to make a stop, she needed a beer. She knew something was up, so he finally told her that they were going to my new restaurant.

Upon arrival, instead of entering the restaurant with him, Mary sneaked in the side entrance and sat at the bar. Meanwhile, Jerry came in the front door, and I was waiting to greet him. I gave him a tour of the entire restaurant and then we went to the bar and there

Above photo: Jerry Thirion, Mary and I.

was Mary. It was nice to see her again. We made another date, and another date, and another date…

While we dated, Mary normally drove up to Pinellas County because the restaurant was closed on Wednesdays. She would arrive Tuesday night and go back to Sarasota early Thursday mornings.

On one particular occasion, I had gone down to Sarasota to stay with her. I woke up at 5:00 am the next morning with excruciating back pains. I couldn't move in any way to get relief. So I got dressed and decided to drive home so I could crawl into my hole. Mary was still half asleep but asked what she could do to help me. I replied that I needed to go home as my doctors were there.

As I was driving over the Sunshine Skyway, the pains were coming in waves. When I drove up to the toll booth, I was complaining to the operator that I was in so much pain.

And she responded, "You have yourself a kidney stone!"

I told her I couldn't drive anymore so she told me to pull over, and they called an ambulance for me.

They put me on a stretcher and during the ride, the waves of pain just kept coming and coming. I finally yelled, "Step on it and turn on the bubble gum machine and the sirens!" They finally got moving, and as I requested, took me to Morton Plant Hospital in Clearwater, where all my doctors were. They brought me into the ER, put me on a bed and pulled the curtains closed.

I felt like a prisoner; no window, no one was there. I was in real pain and they hadn't given me anything or even looked in on me. They were trying to get a hold of my primary doctor but he was a running a marathon. So, finally I got up out of bed, got dressed and ripped open the curtains.

A nurse came in and asked, "Where are you going."

I replied, "I'm going to see a veterinarian, you guys don't take care of me."

The nurse insisted that I lie down again, which I did. Finally, Dr. Ross came in, a urologist. (I ended up being his longest patient, over 42 years). He confirmed that I had a kidney stone, and that they needed to get me up to X-ray. Upstairs, they finally gave me something for the pain, and then I was in happy land.

This event really made me consider my relationship with Mary. I wished she had been with me. I don't know if we were ever engaged.

Every November, I attended the New York Hotel Show in Lincoln Center, and I would stay in nice hotels like The Plaza. At the same time, there was an annual reunion for Cornell graduates. Since Mary had never been to New York City, in November 1977 I brought her to the show. I took her to Tiffany's; she chose her engagement ring and I chose my wedding band for when we did get married.

We didn't announce anything because Mary had to talk to her parents first, and she wanted to go home to Pittsburgh and stay for three months. I flew up every so often to visit. I finally did ask Mary's father for her hand in marriage.

CHAPTER 11

HONEYMOON WITH MARY (AND HER PARENTS)

Our church service took place in Pittsburgh on January 7, 1978 with the wedding reception following at the University Club. About 100 people or so attended, consisting mostly of her family. My mother and one of her Hungarian friends attended as she was in the States at the time visiting. I invited a number of my friends from Cornell...Gert, Udo and others, and my partner, Karl. Our priest was a Presbyterian minister, Dr. Cromie.

For our honeymoon night, we stayed at Mary's parent's home in Mary's room and her sister, Beth, was across the hall. Mary had been so stressed about the wedding and was exhausted that evening. So she went to bed and fell asleep immediately while I stayed up, reflecting on the events of the day. I recall a heavy thunderstorm that night with lots of lightning. I looked over at Mary and saw that she had a smile on her face. I thought she was awake but then loud thunder woke her, and she opened her eyes.

*Above photo: Our wedding day photograph on
January 7, 1978.*

I asked, "Why are you smiling?"

She replied that she had been dreaming about the reception and the many pictures that had been taken of us; she was just smiling for the camera.

The next morning, we got up and planned to spend a few days taking the back roads from Pittsburgh back to Florida. It was very cold and with all the rain from the night before, there was lots of ice on the ground.

Mary's parents' home had a long driveway to the garage with a steep decline. As I began to drive up, Mary told me to stop as her mother, in a bathrobe, was running out of the house. Her mother came over to the car, waving something in her hand. She came up to my window and said, "Just a moment, I forgot to give Mary the car payment booklet, and here it is."

I was now paying for her monkey yellow Oldsmobile, packed with all of her things. That was a memorable moment for me.

Our first night, we drove to White Sulphur Springs, West Virginia to stay in a beautiful cottage on the property of the Greenbrier Hotel. I happened to know the General Manager who originally started in Tampa. We learned that beneath the mountain there is a bunker with offices and living spaces to safely house the U.S. President, Congress and their staff in case of a major nuclear attack.

After a few days in West Virginia, we stopped for one night at a bed and breakfast in the small community of Little Switzerland, North Carolina. It was the only place available to stay that actually had sheets on the bed. I wouldn't take my shoes off on the shag rug and just knew that the bedspread moved all by itself! After the events of the marriage, and its upcoming responsibilities, I needed a drink. They had a restaurant too, sort of, but no bar since it was located in a dry county. The receptionist told me that if I really wanted alcohol, they had a guy that would drive to the next town and get us some moonshine. So, I paid the guy to get some moonshine, a new experience for me. It tasted like gasoline.

The next morning, we drove home to Florida. It was the winter, high season for Bon Appétit, so we had to get back. We decided that when business slowed down in the summertime, we would go on an extended honeymoon to Europe.

Mary's father had been to Europe during his Army days. He was a mechanical engineer who owned a business in Pittsburgh called Hydraulic Hose and Fittings. He sold all kinds of hoses and fittings for commercial equipment needed in multiple industries. He was a good customer of a company called, Rexroth, with headquarters located in Ulm, Germany. He thought our honeymoon would be a great opportunity to visit Rexroth and meet the people there.

On the other hand, Mary's mother had never been to Europe. She had heard many stories from her family, who came from Europe, that you shouldn't drink their water and that you had to be careful with some of their food as well.

Long story short, we decided to bring Mary's parents along on our honeymoon to Europe. I booked the flights and arranged for a VW bus because my mother-in-law's six pieces of luggage would not fit in any car. She had packed water bottles and food in case we got really hungry. Our first stop was Ulm, Germany where we walked around the town while Mary's father visited the Rexroth company.

We then drove through Germany to arrive in Austria, my home country. We started out in Innsbruck and stayed in the first hotel I had worked in, the Hotel Europa. Across the street was Hotel Europa, owned by the same company, a bank. In the wintertime, I worked in Hotel Europa and in the summertime, Hotel Tyrol, which was the only time it was open. It was the newer and taller of the two hotels and had a great location in town, near the railroad train station. It was also right down the street from the local bordello, so... a great location. Hotel Tyrol is where I finished my apprenticeship many years earlier because I was "disengaged." The

Executive Housekeeper, who was not Viennese friendly, brought me to such a dangerous mental state that I had no other option other than to slap her face. This caused my "disengagement."

After my disengagement from Hotel Tyrol, I moved on to work at the Park Hotel Mirabel in Salzburg, which was our next destination after Innsbruck. We stayed at the Park Hotel Mirabel, which has since been torn down and replaced with a newer hotel. We took in the sights and sounds of Salzburg for a couple of days and then continued on towards Vienna on the autobahn.

To understand the comedy of my next memory, it's important to understand that every time I went to Pittsburgh to spend time with Mary's parents, her mother took me all around their town and very proudly pointed out where Mary had gone to high school, which was ranked the 7th best in the country. I was given a tour of her high school—here is the gymnasium, here is the library, etc. She would do this Every. Single. Time. Proudly showing off this "fantastic" school.

Back to the honeymoon. It was a Sunday with sunny blue skies in the early afternoon. We were about half way to Vienna when I was driving past the city of Melk, home to Melk Abbey. There atop the town, majestically overlooking the Danube River, stood my boarding school where I had attended for eight years.

As we drove by, I heard my mother-in-law say, "Oh my Lord, what is that?" She was pointing to Melk Abbey.

In reply to my mother-in-law's question, I replied offhandedly, "Oh that? That's my high school!" We didn't stop; we went onto Vienna, my hometown, my place of birth.

By the time we arrived in the first district of Vienna, it was evening. We quickly learned that it was Messe, an international convention, and no hotel rooms were available. I hadn't thought of planning our stay as I still knew many people in Vienna, particularly in hospitality. I knew there were many more hotels in the second district, which is not that desirable. So, I was driving in our VW bus slowly down a big avenue in the second district that leads to the famous Ferris wheel. As I was driving, I saw in the corner of my eye, a hotel. I turned around and stopped in front. I told everyone to stay in the car while I learned if they had any availability.

When I walked in, there were a number of ladies sitting on sofas in the lobby. I went to the front desk and asked if they had any availability. He replied yes and asked for how long.

"For the night," I replied.

"All night?" was his response.

I assured him I wanted a room for all night to which I heard one of the ladies say, "He must be a pervert." This hotel turned out to be a "Stunden" hotel which means rooms were paid for by the hour.

I continued that I need two adjoining rooms. He said they had a suite with two bedrooms and a connecting door. I told him that would be fine and that I would be right back with the rest of the group. Mary, her mother and father came in. Both Mary and her mother were wearing mink coats. The women on the couches had plenty to say about those coats. We all went straight upstairs to the suite. The first thing we saw coming in was an umbrella stand in a small foyer. To the left was the bathroom, to the right was a door to my in-laws' room and straight ahead was our room. The suite was spotless.

Mary's mother looked around as she hadn't even unbuttoned her mink coat yet. She stood there while my father-in-law undressed and hopped right into bed.

She looked at me and said, "Are you sure we should be here?"

I told her yes, that there was nothing else available and I knew my way around Vienna. She was just concerned about sanitation and finally, slowly started to undress. As far as I was concerned, this had gone on too long, and it was time to go to bed. In my toiletry bag, for whatever reason, I had a prophylactic. I opened it, stretched it out and threw it under her bed.

She was still fussing around when I said, "Look, if you are concerned about sanitation and cleanliness, I'm in the hotel business, the best way to find out what state your room is in, is to look under the bed."

I can still hear that bone-chilling piercing scream! That's when she got up, put her mink coat back on and slept with her clothes on for the night. Mary told her mother what I had done, but could not convince her. I don't think Mary tried that hard; she thought it was funny too.

In the morning, we got up, dressed and left. Needless to say, we only spent one night in Vienna. However, after driving for about 20 miles, I remembered that I had left my beloved Burberry raincoat in the armoire of the suite. Mary wasn't fond of my raincoat, but I still turned back and got my raincoat.

Our next stop was Baden bei Wein, about 25 kilometers outside of Vienna, where my father once lived after his divorce from my mother. Upon arrival, the first thing my father-in-law and I wanted to do was take a shower. There is a beautiful spa in Baden bei Wein that I used to frequent as a child. It is still as nice today as it was in my childhood memory. My father-in-law and I bonded in the sauna, naked, sitting on our towels next to each other.

After Baden bei Wein, we drove back and stayed in a little hotel in the village of Melk. I eventually did take my in-laws on a tour of my "high school," Melk Abbey, and had them meet Abbott Burkhard Ellegast. We drove through Salzburg to Munich, stayed in Erding for a night, and then flew back home. We had been in Europe for three weeks, and I know my in-laws really loved the trip, writing in their journals every day.

CHAPTER 12

TRANSFORMING JAMAICA INN TO BEST WESTERN YACHT HARBOR

Back in 1978, the Jamaica Inn next door to Bon Appétit was owned by a family from Pittsburgh, who coincidentally were next-door neighbors to Mary's parents in Mount Lebanon, a suburb of Pittsburgh. They also owned a residential garbage collection business. The couple had five children; one daughter, Mary, who was widowed, lived alone in the hotel, and operated it with her sister, Jeanie, who lived nearby with her family. Jeanie's husband handled all the maintenance for the hotel and restaurant, and they employed five or six maids that lived nearby. Their son worked with his father in maintenance also but, he knew about as much as I did about maintenance, which isn't saying much. He also worked as a police volunteer. Both ladies were very nice and we became friendly since I often dropped off cookies for them, which they really appreciated.

Above photo: Hotel right next to Bon Appétit that shares parking lot.

As I recall, at that time, a room for up to four people rented for $21.00 per night. Each room had a small kitchenette and a beautiful view of the water.

After negotiating with Mr. Wallace to lengthen our lease, I then approached Mary and Jeanie, with the idea that Bon Appétit and their hotel really should be one business, and asked them to consider selling the hotel to Karl and me. Their hotel lease payment was $2,600 monthly or 6% of gross revenues, whichever was greater. I convinced them to sell, and we bought the Jamaica Inn. Our first year owning the hotel, we never paid the lesser amount.

We did not locally promote our ownership of the Jamaica Inn for the first 10 years because it was so dilapidated and we were embarrassed. Our rooms were pitiful though they were large and clean. So I advertised them with what we did have, water views and good room rates.

Every year I attended the International Tourism Board (ITB), where I promoted not only the Jamaica Inn but also Bon Appétit. European travelers are used to paying a single rate for the number of people that a room can accommodate. So I told international visitors that our rooms were $44 per night for up to four people. And they bought that like hot dinner rolls! Although one time, this guy said to me, "That's got to be a junky place, $44, who would only charge $44, it couldn't be clean." I replied, "No, it's clean. It's just value for your money."

As an exhibitor at ITB, I had to wear these big name tags where your name could be seen from a good distance. Our names were printed in large capital letters. The next line was which state you were from, followed by the city. The last line was the name of the hotel, in bold letters again. Therefore my tag read, "PETER, Florida, Dunedin, JAMAICA INN." So, I would be walking down the halls and people would say, "Hey, Jamaica Man". I did not like that, so by the next ITB, we had changed the name to Inn on the Water. Though the hotel is located on St. Joseph's Sound Bay, I didn't want

Inn on the Bay but, instead, wanted to emphasize that we were on the water because it sounded different. We didn't choose Inn on the Ocean either because we were hundreds of miles away from the ocean, so...truth in advertising.

Inn on the Water was a temporary fix. Everybody asked if we were on the beach and I would respond that the beach was three miles to the north, or three miles to the south, on beautiful Gulf of Mexico. The short answer should have been, "No, we're not on the beach" but I didn't want to say, "No", because we never say no to our guests. Eventually we changed the name to Yacht Harbor Inn which took care of most of the "Are you on the beach?" questions but, we still had a lot of work to do with the hotel property.

Over the first four to five years of ownership, we made interior improvements to the property out of cash flow. The majority of the rooms had kitchenettes, which were used by most of our northern guests. In addition to all the food smells, guests left the pots and pans for the maids to clean. It was a mess, so the first thing we did was rip out the kitchenettes. Besides, we had a great restaurant next door, they didn't need to cook!

Sometime in the 1980's, we decided that maybe a franchise hotel would help us with vacancies. From traveling around the country, my impression of Best Western was really negative. All I remembered were their flashing neon signs on the highway. I used to ask myself who in the world would want to sleep there; you can't even fall asleep with those flashing lights. But in my research, I purchased an industry journal that listed and compared all of the hotel franchises. At that time, the minimum commitment to sign with a franchise (like Marriott, Sheraton, Holiday Inn), with no negotiation, was 20 years. I didn't want to marry any organization for 20 years! And, whether we liked it or not, we would have had to pay additional fees for marketing and advertising. It was very expensive and we only had 54 rentable units.

Then I saw the information on Best Western. For our size and number of rooms, it was $21,000 a year and we could cancel at any time. I nearly jumped over my own shadow! I was willing to risk that. The $21,000 a year was all inclusive with no extra fees for marketing and advertising. Even if we closed the hotel, we were only obligated to pay for the first year. So I told Karl about it, and we agreed to go ahead. We signed up for one year because we had nothing to lose. Our improvements helped us to qualify to Best Western standards, and in the first year, we collected $250,000 in new revenue through their reservation system. It proved to be a good move and I became a big fan of Best Western.

Once our name was changed to Best Western Yacht Harbor Inn, if anybody asked, are you on the beach, I said, "No, but we're on the marina and on the water". Though we had Bon Appétit next door, we continued to focus on the hotel because the restaurant was a given; once guests arrived, they could easily see the restaurant. As a result, Best Western always called us a restaurant with rooms, rather than a hotel with a restaurant. By the way, that turned out to be a negative for us sometimes. Hotel restaurants are typically losers so guests assumed Bon Appétit was not good and always asked for recommendations to good restaurants. We had to encourage them to look at our menu before they went somewhere else.

Once a part of the Best Western franchise, I attended their international conventions. The first year I attended, they had an incredible attorney presenting. He was a New York lawyer that sued hotels and made a fabulous living doing so. I recall him saying that if you don't charge enough, people will stay away from your place. Traveling on any major highway, there is a hotel on every corner at each exit. With four hotels to choose from, one is $25 a night, one is $27 a night, one is $29 a night, and the last one is $48 a night. He asked us, "Where would you stay?" He guessed that most people would stay at the hotel for $48 a night. His point was that we weren't charging enough. Another comment the attorney made was that unless our guests were shouting and slamming their fist at check-out, saying, "This is ridiculous for what you charge!", then we were not charging enough. Obviously these comments stuck in my mind, so much so, that upon my return home, we changed our rates from $44 to $64 a night. Not one guest ever complained about the increased rate; it was still a good value.

Our positive experience as a Best Western franchise encouraged me to get involved with the corporate side too. At that time, I felt Best Western was more like a condo association rather than a franchise since membership gave everyone a vote. We had 2,000 hotels and not even three hotel owners could agree. So, we were always eight to 10 years behind the rest of the industry. That of course reflected in our hotels. Plus there were lots of personal associations within the membership, lots of cliches. I was pretty outspoken so they asked me, if I had a better way, why didn't I run for a Governor position. So, I did, and won. As Governor, I covered all of Florida with about 130 hotels. Our district also included the Bahamas, Georgia, Alabama, and Mississippi, and was led by Paula V.

My responsibilities were one, to look out for Best Western and, two, I had to annually visit every Best Western hotel in the state of Florida, from the Keys all the way to the Panhandle. Initially, I would meet with the owner or general manager and point out whatever shortcomings I found in a constructive manner.

Over time, I wanted Karl to also know what was going on with Best Western so I invited him to join me in Tulsa, OK. We had adjacent rooms and when I walked into mine, the carpet was so filthy that it sucked the shoe right off my foot! I definitely shared that event at the next international meeting! The owner of this hotel was on the Board of Directors. I had talked to a lot of different owners and staff within the corporate organization, and everybody agreed with me, that our standards had to be consistent. The problem was that Best Western was a membership run organization. The owners made the rules so, I felt, the members of the Board of Directors looked out for themselves, and their friends because that's who had voted them in as a Director.

As I mentioned earlier, Best Western had 2,000 hotels in this country, and each one was individually built, owned and operated. In comparison, one competitor in the same price category, Holiday Inn, had a motto, "The Best Surprise is No Surprise." Holiday Inn guests knew that if they rented a room there, it would have a three piece bathroom with a sink outside of the shower and toilet room, and that they offered a restaurant on premise. At a Best Western, guests had no idea what to expect.

We had some real dogs in Best Western but then we had some very nice properties, most of them west of the Mississippi, where they had started. Our hotels in Oregon, Washington, and Montana would elicit a comment like, "God, this is beautiful", compared to the garbage we had in the east.

As a Governor, I had the opportunity to work with Best Western corporate, which sometimes meant the Board of Directors. At one convention, I suggested that all of us member hotels get together and decide on putting our hotels into two different categories. I knew all the owners would never ever see eye to eye. For example, Idaho had 80 hotels and some of them were really spectacular and could be in the Best Western Plus (BWP) category. While others were okay and could remain a Best Western. Each owner could make their own decision but, had to pass an inspection, with scores related to certain standards in sanitation, safety, and the condition of the furnishings to become a BWP.

This concept is called segmentation and we struggled with it for years. I became a pariah as I wouldn't let the concept die. Around that time, Best Western hired Bill W as the new Sr. VP in Sales & Marketing; he had previously worked at Pan Am for a long time.

I approached Bill with the concept. I explained that for an extra $100 a month, owners could choose to become segmented into BWP and that he, Bill, could represent us. He thought it was a great idea, thinking that maybe other hotel owners would see the light. BWP, with a $1.8 million annual budget, could have their own advertising budget and pay Bill separately. I told him that I already won a 1,000 votes from all of the European properties. In contrast, I only received about 500 of the 2,000 American hotel owners because most wanted the status quo. They did not like the segmentation concept since they didn't have to meet any current standards and didn't want to spend more money on their properties.

Those of us that were on board with this concept hired our own attorney because Best Western had theirs. We were doing what we were allowed to do since it was a membership association and every member had a vote. Bill supported me 100% in what I was trying to do. Our District Manager, Paula, was going to join us as well, all within Best Western.

The word got out. We were in London actually and we had everything we needed. Those that wanted segmentation had agreed to pay $1,200 a year, which was peanuts. Paula and I went to him, and said, "Here, take this and spend the money how you see fit under the Best Western Plus brand." We had everything signed, sealed and delivered, and then Bill got cold feet. I was so surprised; we had given him everything on a silver platter. Bill was freshly married, had a child with a disability, and I think, felt too much pressure too soon.

Well, the segmentation concept didn't go anywhere while we owned the hotel. Karl never liked the hotel because he was in charge of its maintenance, and it was maintenance intensive. I liked owning it because I traveled to ITB and met people from all of the world. Some of these new friends would come to Dunedin, stay at our hotel, eat at Bon Appétit, and we formed lasting friendships. We finally decided to sell the Best Western Yacht Harbor Inn in 2010. Though we never listed it, it sold quickly.

Today Best Western has more than seven segmentation brands, one being Best Western Plus; an idea I came up with in the 1980's.

My mother and I (about 12–13 years old) while I was at school at Melk Abbey

My father and me next to his fancy car.

My mother and father on their wedding day

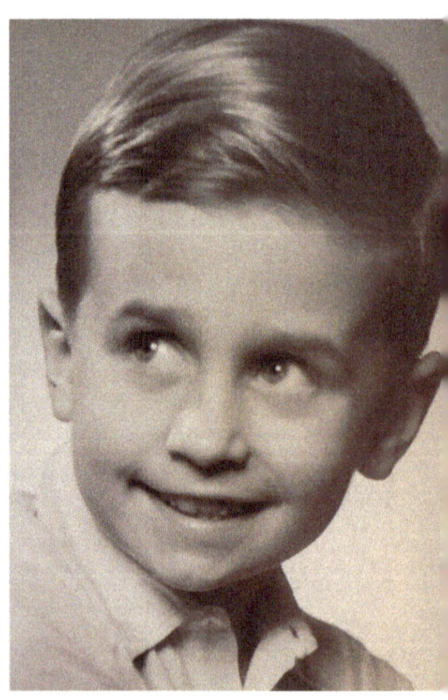

At eight years old.

My elementary class in Grinzing, in the 19th district of Vienna, Austria.

My paternal grandmother and I visiting.

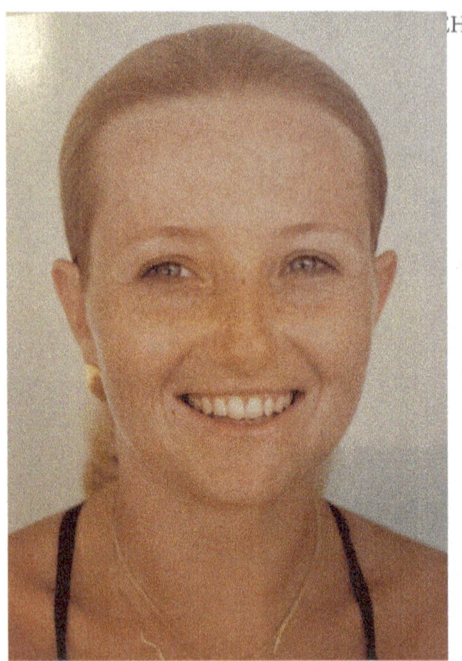

Mary, when I first met her at the
Colony Beach & Tennis Resort

Mary, Casey and Courtney

Casey and Courtney

Mary's parents.

Karl and I working at
Bon Appétit in the
early days.

My mother, Mary and Mary's mom on our wedding day.

CHAPTER 13

CHANGE PAYS OFF

When Karl and I started the restaurant business together, we agreed to separate responsibilities by our strengths. I had a degree in Hotel Management from Cornell, so I handled the front of house and administration. Karl was a highly trained chef, so he ran the back of house, and managed all renovations and additions to Bon Appétit. Every year, I went skiing in Colorado, and I saw what they did with outdoor terraces and how nice it was to sit in the sun after a long day of exercise. I came back one year and told Karl we should build a terrace at Bon Appétit and make a provision for rain. Our first attempt had a metal roof with plastic roll-down walls for when it rained. In the early 1980s, we ultimately hired an architect who designed the terrace as it is now.

When we first opened Bon Appétit, we wanted to be the best restaurant possible. In the first 10 years in a row, we were 4-star rated. But then we realized that what we really wanted to be was the most popular restaurant, and that's why we have made so many changes; we listened to what our guests wanted.

Above photo: The waterfront terrace at Bon Appétit.

My "uniform" used to be a blazer with a shirt and tie every day.

One day, a customer came up to me and said, "When will get rid of your blazer? You make me uncomfortable. I come here with short sleeves."

I responded, "Thank you for pointing that out." After that day, I never put on another blazer again.

When we opened, men were required to wear coat and tie, and women had to wear dresses. Our waiters were in tuxes and wore white gloves, served chilled forks with our salads; it was the European touch. It was new to Americans and not necessarily embraced. They didn't really like a cold fork and often asked for a regular one. These small touches set us apart from other restaurants, but we realized only a small minority of people appreciated them.

While we offered a fine dining ambiance in our first 10 years of business, we quickly became known as a special occasion restaurant to celebrate birthdays, anniversaries, etc. In the early days, Dunedin was more of a blue-collar community, and we realized it was not in our best interest to stick with our high-end uniforms because there were a limited number of people that wanted to eat in fancy clothing. So in 1986 we made the decision to become the "most popular" restaurant. We changed the server uniforms to khaki pants/shorts and white shirts. The following 12 months after changing the concept, we grew revenues by $1 million dollars. While Bon Appétit is still known as a special occasion restaurant, our guests know that they can come casually dressed.

Bon Appétit has an amazing second floor with floor to ceiling windows that provide gorgeous views of St. Joseph's Sound and breathtaking sunsets. We wanted to continue to use the second floor for events, but after July of 1990, when the Americans with Disabilities Act (ADA) was signed into law, we were out of compliance. We did not have an elevator.

I drove to Orlando to meet with the ADA Board of Florida. The Board was made up of 10 or 12 people that, with one exception, were in wheelchairs. My purpose for attending was to file for an exception so that we did not have to install an elevator. My argument was that all of the board members could come to Bon Appétit and sit at a table that was much closer to the water than the second floor. I also added that not all people in a wheelchair needed one all the time. I was sensitive to their plight as my own mother was confined to a wheelchair toward the end of her life. Long story short, I was approved. Without their requirement, we did have a wheelchair lift installed at the front of the building that takes wheelchair-bound guests to the second floor. We also added an indoor lift that takes our wheelchair-bound guests up three steps to the restrooms.

Several former employees of Bon Appétit have gone on to open their own restaurant businesses. We hired Patti at Bon Appétit, whose father was our HR Manager at Innisbrook. She opened a restaurant after working for us.

Then, we had Anthony, who married our front office girl at our hotel, who opened an Asian restaurant on 580 and then another one near Safety Harbor.

Mario, who owned the Country Boy restaurant in Dunedin and built that whole shopping center, was once a waiter with us.

I think most people want to get ahead and want to grow. But I would say that's the American spirit. You have to change, you have to welcome change, you have to create change in order to grow.

In the 47 years we had owned Bon Appétit, it went through several renovations, usually every four to six years. The last one was completed in 2018 with the addition of the outside bar, Marina's Café. During the pandemic, the outdoor space was what kept us open to guests, allowing us to continue employment for our associates and thriving in an extraordinary business climate. The only major change was that we had to discontinue valet service.

CHAPTER 14

TEACHING AT CORNELL

In early 1984, I was sitting in my office, looking at the mudflats. Bon Appétit had been open for nearly 6 years and I had hardly traveled, so I was feeling restless. I started thinking, "What am I doing here?" So, I called my friend, Gert, who was now the Dean of Students at Harvard University.

I said, "Gert, I'm coming to New England. I'm going to take 10 days and drive through New Hampshire, Maine, and maybe Vermont. I'm going to see New England."

He said, "I'll go with you," and he did.

During the trip, I said, "You know, at the end of our trip, before I go back to Florida, I want to stop in Ithaca and go to Cornell again. I can see my professors there."

While on campus, we ran into the Assistant Dean, Colonel Gaurnier, who was an Army officer in his previous career. Gert was with me, and he knew that we were always up to no good. He said, "What are you guys doing here?"

I told him that I actually wanted to move to New England, specifically to Portsmouth, New Hampshire. I had found a house and a restaurant. I wanted a seasonal climate, four seasons, not just the summer.

The professor said, "Aren't you in Florida with a place on the water?"

I said, "Yes."

"Well, what are you going to do with it?" he asked.

I replied, "Give it to my partner. I want to do something on my own in this area."

That's when the professor said, "I have a suggestion for you. Next semester, I'm going on sabbatical. You take my courses that I teach at the Hotel School."

Then I said, "Well, I would have to move up here."

"Get a house," he replied so he helped me lease a house from a law professor who was also on sabbatical.

I planned for Mary and the girls to move up to Ithaca for one semester. But then my mother's medical condition was deteriorating, and she needed a lot of attention with doctors and aides coming and going. Mary volunteered to stay home and keep an eye on her. Instead I commuted for a whole semester from Tampa to Ithaca; I would leave on Wednesday and came back Friday night. I taught two graduate courses: one in Hotel Administration and one in Restaurant Administration. The undergraduate course was in Business Development.

What really soured me on teaching was that I flew 4,000 miles a week, and some of the Hotel School students couldn't bother to make it to class from their dorm room. It was disgusting. You know, when I was a student at Cornell, I paid so much money, I wouldn't miss an hour. But that's not the case anymore.

One girl never came to my class. Her father had given $20 million to the University, and she didn't come to school. Guess what? I flunked her. After the semester, the Dean called me and wanted to talk to me about her.

I told him, "I have nothing to say, I never met her. She was enrolled in my class but never came to class. To be fair to everyone else, I had no choice but to give her an F."

The Dean hemmed and hawed and said, "Yes, but her father is a big supporter of the school."

I responded, "With all due respect, I paid for my tuition at Cornell. I value my degree, if you give this girl a passing grade, then you cheated me out of my money." I never followed up. I don't know if he changed her grade and I didn't want to know. I had paid too much for my education.

My education opened up the whole world to me. I could do whatever I wanted, wherever I wanted. I could have gone to China, Japan, Africa, Europe, and North America, anywhere in the world. There were plenty of positions available for what I was qualified to do. And every week, I got the bulletin that listed jobs all over the world once I graduated. The bulletin listed positions that needed to be filled with all the information as to salary and benefits, like hotel accommodations with meals and maid service, and a vehicle. These opportunities came from alumni that went back home and were looking to fill positions needed for their hotels, restaurants, steamship companies, whatever. They went back to their Alma Mater. It wasn't just about the education but also about the connections made. We are in the people business.

While teaching the students that semester, I felt the same optimism for them that I had for myself. But I learned that teaching was not my passion. Number one, I felt that some of the students were so disrespectful. Number two, I felt parents were being cheated out of their money. Tuition was always expensive and it was going to waste because their kids were not showing up for class. I was flying

4,000 miles a week, every week for a semester. I had a different attitude when I was in school; I felt privileged to attend an Ivy League university.

CHAPTER 15

THE STORY OF CAFÉ ALFRESCO

I was still at Innisbrook when East Lake Woodlands was being developed by Alan R. There were no signs or any indication of what was being built on this large piece of property that looked initially like a resort so close to Innisbrook. Ultimately, we became good friends with Alan, and his wife, Ingrid, who was from Sweden. We learned later that they developed a country club setting with single family homes, condos, and a tennis club. Mary and I joined the tennis club and met lots of people there. Every Sunday, they held tennis tournaments, and that's where we met one couple, Harry L. and his wife, Sue. He was a very good tennis player with a 4-plus rating.

We didn't talk much about our careers but later I discovered that he was the President of Eckerd Drugstores. They lived in Belleair, in walking distance from our home. For the holidays, particularly Christmas, Sue always invited us to come to their Christmas party with their family, friends and neighbors. Now, I had no idea of how old Harry was, but I knew that he was extremely physically fit and looked really young to me.

We attended their Christmas party for many years, but one year, Sue said to me, "You know what Peter, Harry is retiring and I don't know what to do with him all day. I need to get him out of the house."

I responded, "Well, I have something for Harry to do! Harry is the only Greek person that I know in America who is not in the restaurant business." I told her that we had just bought property in Dunedin and needed to develop it.

So, that's how my association started with Harry. Months earlier, I had seen a sign in the window of a little white building on Main Street that said, "For Sale by Owner." I parked, walked in and asked for the owner. The woman behind the counter was deaf and could only communicate by writing and reading lips.

"I'm the owner," she said.

I pointed to the sign and said, "I want to buy it."

"When?" she asked.

"Now," I replied, and we arranged to sign contracts shortly thereafter.

Around the time Harry retired, I was trying to buy the vacant lot next to the little building I already owned. The lot was filled with garbage, in fact, the whole of downtown Dunedin was a mess. The property was owned by Sun Bank, (now Truist) where I did our business banking, and I knew most everyone.

So, one afternoon, Harry and I were discussing this situation. I mentioned that at that time on every street corner in New Orleans, they had "snowballs" which were crushed ice in a cup that are then drizzled with flavorings and alcohol. It was a great summertime dessert. Harry thought it was a good idea to offer it in downtown Dunedin since the weather was warm, like in New Orleans. We wanted to open several locations along the Pinellas Trail but Pinellas County wouldn't approve the permits because it would set a precedent, and then everyone else would want to open similar businesses along the Trail.

About the same time, I was still in negotiations with Sun Bank about the lot. I approached them again, and told them I wanted to buy the lot. They again said the lot is not for sale.

I replied, "What do you mean not for sale? Everything is for sale. Right now, it's a garbage dump!" Again, they said no, unless I bought the entire city block, it all went together.

I asked, "What am I going to do with an entire block along the trail and a warehouse?"

They replied, "That's your decision." We eventually bought all of it, and thus I got the empty lot.

With the warehouse, I was thinking of putting in a little sidewalk café with outdoor seating, overlooking the Pinellas Trail. But I had no idea what to do with the rest of it. I asked Harry if he had any ideas about the building. He responded no, but that he knew someone that may, and that was Bob T, who owned a large construction company, was an architect and consultant. Bob built the first 32 Publix and Eckerd Drug stores for his personal friend, Jack Eckerd, and the Jenkins family who owned Publix.

Bob was a real gentleman, Mr. Clearwater and the Commodore of the Carlouel Yacht Club many times. He was very well respected and fun to spend time with. I introduced Bob to Bill of Beaux-Arts Group, an architectural firm in downtown Tampa. They also sold high-end executive furniture.

Bob came out and drew up the plans to modify the warehouse into Café Alfresco and the storefronts that are there today. My partner, Karl, and I purchased the whole block initially and later included Harry and Les R., who was the Executive VP at Eckerd. Bill did all the architectural work, and we purchased the furniture in line with my vision of a real European sidewalk café. Karl was not initially in favor of putting another restaurant on the Pinellas Trail, but I felt it would be the catalyst for the success of the entire development, and it was important to do it right. I went to several coffee companies to lease the space but couldn't find the right fit. Finally, I went to Karl and said that we needed to do it ourselves, so we did. Now Harry was really engaged, and we worked well together.

As Café Alfresco was under construction, storefronts were also being built and leased quickly. After the first year of operation, each investor was paid back their initial investment and no longer had any risk. Eventually, the property was completed, Café Alfresco opened, and it remains virtually the same as it began.

Harry came for lunch at the café once or twice a week and helped with other business too. While we sat eating, people would stop by the table to say hello.

I would introduce Harry to them, "This is Harry, and he is the President of Eckerd Drugs, a multi-million-dollar company." I wanted to make sure he felt respected.

Harry would respond. "You mean, a multi-billion-dollar company, don't you Peter?"

Harry's wife, Sue, loved North Carolina so they had a large, beautiful home built on the top of the mountain. She lived there nearly full-time whereas Harry commuted back and forth, spending his summers there full-time. As smart and as gifted as he was, we shared something in common… we were not handy. As a side bar, for 20 years, we owned and I operated the US *Bon Appétit* that I will talk about later. I took care of the engine room because I was interested in it. I am not interested in hammers and nails.

Mary and I went to visit Harry and Sue in their home in Waynesville, North Carolina. It had a big entrance and gate, a foyer, large living room, formal dining room and I don't know how many bedrooms, and a large garage.

We came back into the house and Harry walked me over to a room with a window with a beautiful view, and I asked Harry, "What is this room?"

He replied, "It's my workshop." There was nothing in there except a hammer, a screwdriver and a wrench on a table, along with a bicycle pump, which belonged to his wife for her bike. He had a great sense of humor too.

Unfortunately, Harry developed some medical issues and ultimately passed away. He was buried at the Episcopal Church of the Ascension in downtown Clearwater where we all used to attend when we lived in Belleair. We miss him dearly to this day.

After the property development was all done, Bob T. continued to be a frequent guest at Bon Appétit and Café Alfresco. After his divorce, he was the most eligible bachelor in Pinellas County. He reminded me of my friend Jerry Thirion from the Colony who had women chasing after him. Bob originally had an office on Myrtle Avenue in Clearwater, but I asked him to move into an office with us in the Dunedin Chamber building. He came to work every day until 5:00 p.m. and then drove himself home. He still had connections in South Florida, near Lake Okeechobee, where he was building banks. As time went on, ultimately, we were his last client. Bob was always elegantly dressed with snow white hair. I didn't know another person like him.

On Bob's 90th birthday, I told him I knew an extremely wealthy lady that was in love with him. I could see him on his honeymoon cruise around the world, but before he got married and abandoned us, he had to find his replacement. So he brought us Charlie J. Charlie was also a developer with whom Bob had worked with in the past.

One Monday a neighbor of his, who was a retired nurse, called me to say that Bob wasn't feeling well that day but would be in the office the next day. She called again on Tuesday, stating it was still too early for him to return to work. Wednesday and Thursday, the same thing.

Charlie had purchased and developed many lots in Highlands, North Carolina. The economy had taken a downturn so he wanted to move back to Florida. Charlie was in town that Friday of the week that Bob was calling in sick. When I saw Charlie, I suggested that we visit Bob in his Belleair home. When we arrived, Bob was looking pretty good and was sharp of mind, despite having a hospice nurse there to take care of him. He asked why we had come, and we explained that we wanted to check up on him and see if he needed anything. He kept repeating to me that we needed to buy some other properties in Dunedin that we had determined was a good investment. Even as sick as he was, he was still thinking about business. After a short visit, the nurse asked us to leave.

The next day, Saturday, Karl, Charlie and I went to visit Bob again. He had noticeably deteriorated but kept bringing up that we needed to make that deal. I chided him, telling him that he needed to think about his health, and not business. He passed away the next morning, June 18, 2012, on Father's Day. After his passing, we kept his architectural filing cabinet that has short, deep drawers where we keep the plans and drawings of our properties.

Bob and Charlie had built many projects together. Bob would design some, and Charlie would build them and vice versa. Before our development was completed, Charlie had approached us to buy us all out. I was not interested in selling so he asked if he could buy into our project. We all went to Orlando to discuss Charlie's request with Harry's son, Bill, who handled financial affairs for his mom, Sue. Together we agreed to sell Charlie 25% because property development was his forte. Since he was now a partner, we wanted to find another investment for diversification. In Charlie's previous career, he had worked for Squire, which did a lot of land development in Hillsborough County and in other areas of Florida. Charlie also knew John C. of JMC Communities, which specialized in condominiums, single-family homes, resorts, and commercial enterprises. On Clearwater Beach, they built Opal Sands, Sand Pearl and the condominiums next to it, the Pelican Golf Club in Belleair, Ovation Condominiums in downtown St. Petersburg, and hundreds of others in several states. They are one of the most respected developers in the country.

Just east of Bon Appétit, there was a large vacant lot facing Main Street that was being developed by JMC. We met with John, and he told us they were going to build 30 condominiums and eight retail spaces downstairs. I asked him if he would consider selling the retail stores, and he responded that it was his intention. So I looked at Charlie and said we should buy them all. He was surprised but agreed. We gave John a down payment without a shovel in the ground. What is now known as Victoria Place has turned out to be a good investment too. All the condominiums were sold before they broke ground.

CHAPTER 16

OUR FAMILY OVER THE YEARS

After putting in my resignation at Innisbrook, I needed to find a place to live, preferably in Dunedin, close to Bon Appétit. It was the first time I needed to buy a place to live in, so I purchased a condominium at Edgewater Arms because it was directly across the marina from the restaurant. It was within walking distance, and that was good. I bought a two-bedroom condominium because I was single at the time.

About a year later, Mary and I got married, and she wanted children, which was unknown territory for me, but she became pregnant shortly thereafter. This condominium project did not allow children, so we sold the condo and moved to the nearby community of Belleair. We bought a large piece of property on a double lot with a two-bedroom, two-bathroom house but renovated it to include a total of five bedrooms and five bathrooms. Both girls were born there. Our first daughter, Courtney, was born July 30, 1979, and our second daughter, Casey, was born October 17, 1981. When I brought my mother from Austria to live with us, we were able to give her a wing of her own that included a small kitchenette.

Above photo: Our family Christmas card, 1981.

She was wheelchair bound and needed a handicap-accessible living space.

I had been visiting her several times a year in Austria to check on her. The medical care I could provide for her in the States was so much better so I decided to move her in with us sometime in mid-1979. It was a difficult time for Mary and my mother. When she moved in, she knew no English, and Mary did not know a word of German. My mother could be a handful so it wasn't long before we thought it best to move closer to the restaurant in Dunedin. I was sometimes making the eight-mile trip up to four times a day.

As the girls became of age to go to school, we decided to move back to Dunedin. Most of our neighbors in Belleair sent their children to private schools. Since I was a product of only private schools, and while they can be very good, I wanted our girls to get a taste of the real world, not the insular environment private schools might provide.

We were fortunate to find someone to purchase our Belleair home immediately. Since we wanted to build our next home, we rented another home in Belleair for a year and half while we hired a wonderful architect from Tampa to build our home on Victoria Drive in Dunedin, within walking distance of Bon Appétit. During the same time frame, I renovated and created an apartment on the second floor of the Best Western, next door to Bon Appétit. Once that was done, we moved my mother into her own suite so I could visit her as often as she needed me. I also hired three people that were available to take care of my mother around the clock. She lived there for five years until her death in 1984.

We loved our home on Victoria Drive, across from St. Joseph's Sound. And though it was a private street, not well known to most people, fishermen in their pick-up trucks would fly down our dirt road along the Sound. I was always worried to death about our two small girls playing outside. I just wanted to get away from that. So, in early 1991, we moved into the home in Dunedin where Mary and I still live today. Mary is a gifted and degreed designer; I have always left the beauty of our home in her very capable hands. It's set way back from the road and was large enough to host all of Courtney and Casey's friends to play safely.

Looking back, I'm very thankful and happy for my girls. I worked hard, seven days a week to make Bon Appétit the most popular restaurant in Dunedin. As the girls grew up and were able to work, they did various jobs at both Bon Appétit and Café Alfresco during their summer breaks. While they were both very conscientious about their work, they never expressed any desire to work in the restaurant business, predominantly because of the number of hours that I was not home. I was never disappointed that they could not see themselves in the restaurant business, even though they work the same number of hours now. Courtney and Casey enjoy their medical careers; it makes them feel good to help people in a different way.

Despite my long work hours, we always shared holiday meals as a family. Sometimes Mary cooked at home, or I brought something from the restaurant. Other times, we ate together at Bon Appétit but then I had to go back to work. I didn't come home every night for meals either. I recall that I came home one day through the back door through the kitchen. Mary was cooking at the time.

Casey was about seven years old and said to me, "You know, Daddy, now I know what you do. You come home and see what mom is cooking and then you say, 'I still have to go back to work.' And then you eat at the restaurant."

Mary was the disciplinarian. For the most part, the girls went to Mary with their troubles but when they had a really big problem, they came to their daddy. As a child, Courtney spent more time with me because I used to take her to Clearwater Beach, when The Pelican was still there. Henry Enriques and his nephew ran that place, and we would have meetings there every Saturday. All the guys would come and have drinks, and Courtney would always come along with me. She wasn't very old, and the only female, so she got a lot of attention. Meanwhile, Casey spent more time at home with her mom.

CHAPTER 17

THE U.S. *BON APPÉTIT*

As an extension to the Bon Appétit restaurant, we purchased a motor yacht, the US *Bon Appétit*, that we used for guest entertainment. The ship was custom built in Newport News in Virginia Beach, entirely made of steel and weighed 67 tons. Its length was 72 feet and had a capacity of 1500 gallons of diesel fuel. The US *Bon Appétit* also had the Devo paint system, the same used on nuclear submarines. Hence, it was an extremely safe vessel.

Everyone in their lives has a special day whether it's a wedding, a divorce, a celebration of life, or anniversary. We had the ship docked right in front of our Bon Appétit restaurant, easily seen through our large windows facing the water. We never had to advertise it as it sold itself with its size and appearance. Our guests often asked if they could charter the boat for special occasions. We had a license for up to 53 people on board, which had to include the Captain, mate, and any other staff needed. There was a lifeboat on top and flotation devices for everyone onboard.

Above photo: The U.S. Bon Appétit.

One day, a nice young man came into the office and wished to book our yacht. I asked, "For how many guests," and he responded, just for himself and a young lady that he wanted to propose to.

I explained the menu with refreshments and told him that we typically cruise the intra-coastal waterways, showing him all the beautiful homes, such as where Elvis Presley's daughter lives and so forth. He loved what he heard, decided on the menu, and paid in advance for two people.

The day came for his cruise. I was the only captain at the time, and I could tell we were going to have a magnificent sunset. I asked him if he wanted me to travel further into the Gulf of Mexico so they wouldn't see other vessels while they enjoyed their meal and viewed the sunset. He agreed, and I instructed my team to give them privacy as he was a rather reserved man. So, we got to the last buoy, and I turned the boat around so that there was nothing between them and the sunset. It was a very romantic setting. We stayed until the sun dipped below the horizon, and then we went back to Dunedin.

After I docked the boat, and my crew was removing the provisions, I asked him if he had proposed.

He replied, "No."

I was surprised and asked him why not. He said he just couldn't ask her. I replied that he had paid a lot of money for a romantic evening. I kept asking him for reasons, and he just kept replying that he just couldn't ask her. I felt really bad for him and offered our bridal suite at the Best Western, which we still owned at the time. He said no, that he had to go home by himself, and he did.

Maybe a month or two later, he came back to book our yacht with the identical arrangements and time. He said he was ready to propose. So again I took them out to the Gulf, gave my crew the same instructions, he and his lady had their champagne and caviar with another beautiful sunset. We went back to Dunedin. I docked the boat and then asked him if he had proposed.

"No," he replied.

I didn't know what to do with him. I felt guilty for taking his money twice now, and he hadn't proposed. So, I gave him a 50% discount on that trip and never saw him again. If I were a betting man, I don't think he ever proposed to her.

Cecil Engelbert, the mayor of Dunedin, also worked for an ice company, Lucky Roberts Refrigeration, on Myrtle Avenue. I saw him on almost a daily basis, not only as mayor, but as a vendor for the restaurant. One day, he came to me, stating that his son's father-in-law had passed away, and the family wanted to charter the boat to spread his ashes. Cecil mentioned that this family didn't have much money. He asked me for a sizable discount. I responded that I couldn't give him a discount as I needed to pay a captain and crew, and for diesel fuel, and that cost me $3,000, without food. I couldn't ask someone to captain this trip for free. His solution was for me to be the captain for this trip. I told him we could conceivably do that but that I had never conducted a funeral before. I also warned him that, according to maritime law, we needed to be at least three miles offshore to spread the ashes. He understood, and we set the date and time.

On the given day, eight immediate family members were onboard. Unfortunately, it was not a pretty day; it was gray and dreary, and raindrops were falling. I headed to the intra-coastal and the waves were high with white caps. It definitely was not a day for boating but perhaps appropriate for a funeral. As we ventured out, the family was on the aft deck, no one was in the salon where I was piloting the boat. After a while, Cecil brought in one of the family members and sat her behind me. She was really sobbing, with tears coming down her face. I was concerned for her so I called Cecil back and suggested that someone should be with this lady as she's really suffering.

He replied, "No, don't worry about her, she's just seasick!"

I did worry, however, because we had nice carpeting in the salon. I told him to take her out to the deck as she would feel much better in the open air.

We passed under the Clearwater bridge towards the open Gulf of Mexico. The waves were now much higher and rocking the boat. Behind me in the salon was a buffet table, with an edge that kept items from falling off. The family had placed the box of ashes on that table, and with the boat's rocking, it was sliding from one side to the other. Cecil brought all the family members into the salon and announced that the captain, meaning me, was now going to open the box and spread the ashes.

So, I invited everyone back out to the aft deck while I asked Cecil, "What do you mean the captain will spread the ashes? I am driving this boat in a storm!"

Cecil ignored my comment and continued to ask me for a knife to open the thick plastic bag containing the ashes. I told him that I did not have a knife. But he insisted, so I went below to the engine room, found a screwdriver and returned to the aft.

Meanwhile, we were only half way towards the buoy and nowhere near where we should have been to spread ashes. Cecil again asked me to help distribute the ashes. I had to remind him that we were in bad weather conditions, and I could not leave the helm. He insisted that it wouldn't take long. Everyone was now on the aft deck, some holding flowers. We were not where we were supposed to be but Cecil said, "Do it."

So, I opened the bag and started spreading them. The ashes were gray in color and floated, which was a bad sign. Along with all the thrown flowers, we had left a trail for the Coast Guard or any other boater to see. On the horizon, I then saw a large fishing vessel speeding towards the bridge because the waters were really getting rough out in the Gulf. Then, I saw a Coast Guard plane heading toward land from the Gulf as well. At this point, I was sure that I was going to lose my license. But then I was saved! That large sport fishing vessel came speeding through the ashes and destroyed the evidence.

As soon as I spread the ashes, I went back to the helm but the boat had turned around because of the wave activity. It was now headed back towards Clearwater. A family member had some extra ashes and decided to spread them, but the direction of the boat combined with the winds, made the ashes come back into the salon. I was covered in ashes, from my hair to the back of my captain's uniform.

On our way back to Dunedin, I docked the boat, and the crew started unloading the boat. Cecil came up to me with a $100 tip. I told him, "Cecil, keep it!" He never did pay me for anything that day.

We continued to get busier and busier, and after 300 or so cruises, I hired four on-call captains. We sometimes had two or three events scheduled on any given day and night, each cruise lasting three hours and then an hour before and after to prepare and clean the ship. We had the US *Bon Appétit* for at least 15 years. Financially, we did extremely well, and had the boat paid off within a couple of years. At one point, we had to have it refurbished and sent it to a shipyard to do so. We had to have collision bulkheads installed on this all-steel boat.

The inside of the boat was outfitted as a salon with comfortable sofas and a table with edges to prevent spills. We had three ovens and refrigerators in the galley. When we cruised, everything was working in the kitchen, all the lights, air conditioning, and one bathroom. We burned 2.3 gallons of diesel an hour, which was highly economical. We had a tank capacity of 1,500 gallons of diesel fuel. We could have gone to Europe and back without refueling. The US *Bon Appétit* was 72 feet in length, had one bedroom with a king-sized bed and private tub. Just to start the engine cost $1,000.

Beside the fuel, there were all kinds of additional expenses such as to pay the captain, the cleaning crew, etc. My uniform was standard issue: white pants, white shirt with four black stripes, designating my captain status. I had obtained my 100-ton license.

We had all kinds of events on that boat. As I stated earlier, everyone has a different reason to splurge or celebrate a special occasion. One day, our sales office had a booked an afternoon trip. At this point in time, I was the only captain but I did have a mate from Peru. He was full-time on the boat; he would paint and clean it up after parties as well as prepare it for events. He would also go with me to Tarpon Springs to fill up the tank with diesel fuel. He was also the person we threw overboard when doing our mandatory training drills for man overboard rescues.

On one occasion, this mate was already on the boat, and I was coming from home after changing into my uniform. Several guests had already arrived. I saw in the parking lot Ferraris, Mercedes and other fancy cars. I wondered what was going on. As I walked toward the dock, I saw a lot of young people, all extremely well dressed, something I hadn't seen before in Dunedin. I went onto the bridge, and started the engines as about 30 guests proceeded on board.

We had lovely food and beverages but I noticed that most of the guests were drinking water or soda. Not much alcohol was being consumed. As I steered the boat from the bridge, guests oftentimes would come up to the bow to ask me questions. On this day, I asked what was the special occasion for the party. One gentleman responded that it was his sister's birthday, and the guests were his colleagues from work.

Shortly thereafter, one of the stewards came running up on the bow, screaming to me that I needed to come down as there was a fight happening. So again, I left the helm and went down. Two girls were fighting, one was pulling the other's long hair, scratching and kicking. I had noticed the aggressive one earlier, she stood out from the rest. In my opinion, she looked like a hooker. The woman with the long hair was the birthday girl.

Upon my arrival, the "hooker" had picked up the cake and threw it at the birthday girl's face. That cake went all over the place. At this point, we had just gone under the Clearwater bridge on our way towards Sand Key. We had to wait for the bridge to be raised since our boat had a 30' dry stack that prevented anyone from smelling the diesel fuel. I thought: what do I do now? This had never happened before.

I decided to pull over near the Clearwater Marina, out of the waterway and called the Coast Guard. I said, "United States Coast Guard, motor vessel US *Bon Appétit* calling United States Coast Guard."

They responded, "This is United States Coast Guard, state your emergency."

I replied, "I have a ship out of control!" They asked for my location which I gave.

They then stated, "Stand-by, sir, we'll be there shortly."

True to their reply, I heard sirens shortly thereafter as the U.S. Coast Guard boat arrived. A Coast Guard officer asked me what was going on, and I explained that the ladies had been fighting. He asked me if I could dock the boat but before I did, I told the officer that I did not want any anyone to leave this boat.

He said, "Okay, no problem."

He asked me to dock and throw them the lines so they could secure our boat. I invited him to come on board and showed him the results of their fighting. Meanwhile, all the men had evacuated to the front of the boat. The officer asked me what I wanted them to do.

I replied, "I want them to pay for the trip, to pay for the cleaning, and I want it paid immediately in cash or credit cards."

The officer looked at the women and said, "Okay, you heard the Captain."

I charged a penalty on top of that too. They all chipped in and proceeded to leave the boat. One of the guys begged me not to call the police, saying they would all be fired. Apparently, they worked at a large national investment firm, headquartered in St. Petersburg. Thus, the fancy clothes and cars. I never did find out why those two women had fought nor how they got from the Clearwater Marina back to our parking lot in Dunedin.

As a Captain, I had the ability to marry couples as well. I wasn't very comfortable doing it so I didn't perform many of them. The rules were the same, we had to go out at least three miles, I read the vows from a document, signed some papers, and my job was done. I charged an extra fee for that service too. You cannot miss an income opportunity if you want to stay in business.

We knew a wonderful gentleman, Mr. McElgin, originally from Pittsburgh, that lived in the Edgewater Arms. He owned a nice boat in the marina and was a licensed sea captain and airline pilot among having other engineering licenses. He was the person that had worked with me to acquire the boat and get it Coast Guard ready. He helped us with whatever was needed for the boat. He told us what needed to be done, how the repairs should be done, usually by a boatyard a few miles away in Tarpon Springs. Mr. McElgin was retired and up in years. He helped me because he enjoyed doing so.

I went to Europe at least twice, sometimes three times, a year, especially when my mother was living there. One year I was in Europe the first time a hurricane was coming to Dunedin while we owned the US *Bon Appétit*. The safest place for a boat during a hurricane is in the water. So, Mr. McElgin took the boat across the intra-coastal waterway and attached the boat to our hurricane anchor of 1,000 pounds. No lines extended from the boat that could chafe, break or get caught with other vessels. Then, he stayed alone on the boat and rode out the hurricane while his wife remained in their condo. Beforehand, Karl prepared provisions for his time on the boat.

Unfortunately, this happened a few times before Karl told me that we couldn't continue this way. I always seemed to be in Europe when hurricanes came, and Karl knew nothing about the boat. So, I decided to look into selling the US *Bon Appétit*. My first resource was Courtney Ross, a friend who owned a wonderful boatyard next to Island Way Grill on Island Estates. He outfitted the Southern Ocean Racing Conference for mega yachts from Europe, Austria, the Bahamas, Bermuda, Acapulco, New Zealand, Australia, and other countries or their crew would come to Clearwater Beach and race from the Skyway Bridge over to Ft. Lauderdale. Courtney arranged the entire event.

Every year we had to take the US *Bon Appétit* out of the water to make repairs, remove barnacles, freshen up the paint, and ready it for Coast Guard inspections. Courtney's boat lift could only raise up to 50 tons, so he and I would take the boat past the Skyway bridge to a very nice boatyard in Bradenton. It was a day's trip, and after 15 years of doing this, I felt it was no longer worth it.

Initially our cruises were four hours long, but because our pricing included unlimited alcohol, many guests returned to our dock very drunk. So, we reduced the cruise time to three hours and raised the price. Guests still came back drunk, just not as drunk as before. Thankfully, we never had an accident or injury onboard.

We never had any mechanical issues either. I really took very good care of the US *Bon Appétit*. At home, I can't use a hammer but as Captain, I was totally responsible for her performance as there was no one else that could do it. But I enjoyed it. Every 100 hours, I had to change all the fluids which, when we were busy, meant nearly every four weeks.

I used the boat for family outings as well. I often took my daughters, Courtney and Casey, and sometimes our dog. We'd go out, I'd drop the anchor, and we would spend the night out there. The girls would go swimming from the platform in the back.

By definition, a ship is a boat that has life boats on board. The Coast Guard informed us that in the case of war here, they would confiscate our boat. It was that solidly built.

A man in Palm Beach bought the boat through a broker. He worked with steel all his life and was in the business of bridge building. He put in every reserve system that was available on a boat. If anything went wrong, there was a backup. He even had it painted Battleship Gray. In fact, Karl, Jerry Thirion and I were coming over a bridge in Palm Beach, when we recognized the boat with its lines, the tower, and crane in the marina. It looked like a warship. Apparently the owner lived on it after it was completely refurbished.

Ten years later, I got a call from the broker that had represented him. She told me that the owner was interested in selling the boat, and if I wanted, he would show it to me in a marina in Savannah, Georgia. So, Courtney and I went up and saw the boat. All the technology that had been installed was intimidating to me. The beauty of the boat had been how simple it was to operate that even I could do it.

We went back to the salon with the owner and his girlfriend. He said, "So, Peter, what do you want to do?"

I answered, "Why do you want to sell it now? This is gorgeous what you have done."

He replied that his girlfriend got seasick and didn't like going out. They had bought a home, and the boat was now just sitting unused in the marina. He asked me if I wanted it. I told him that the way he had it now, I would not be able to afford it. He responded that I shouldn't worry about that and asked if I liked it.

I replied, "Yeah, but it's truly intimidating with what you have done."

Besides, he also mentioned that the license to transport up to 53 onboard was expired. It would take at least six months to obtain. This boat was now more than I wanted for just boating; I would need to make a business out of it again. I didn't understand why he didn't have that license. It was so valuable for what could be done with the boat.

As to price, he offered to sell it back to me for the same price I had sold it to him, if I took it. I said okay, but only if he got it back to the Bon Appétit dock where he had picked it up. And I needed at least six months to buy it, to ensure that it met Coast Guard standards in Florida again. I would pay for the transport back to Dunedin, I would insure it, he would save his monthly docking fee of $600 a month, and have no docking fees at Bon Appétit, and no more worries. He wanted to think about it. After a while, we touched base, and he told me that he had given the boat away, as a donation to a not-for-profit organization for a large write-off on his taxes. Courtney and I tried hard to buy it back but we just could not convince him.

We still get calls today for that boat. There was nothing else like the US *Bon Appétit* in the Tampa Bay area.

CHAPTER 18

MARKETING FOR BON APPÉTIT & BEST WESTERN

Since I was responsible for sales and marketing for Bon Appétit and for Inn on the Water (later Best Western), I attended annual events by the International Tourism Board in Berlin, the World Travel Market in London, and POW WOW in different large cities across the U.S. The purpose was to bring new business to Florida, and more specifically to our restaurants, hotel, and our local state parks. During all of these trips, I collected hundreds of business cards and used them when I took my cruise around the world. When I was in Singapore, I had a name and hotel connection, and the same for China and Vietnam, and so on. It wasn't a bad gig; in fact, it was fun.

Pinellas County had a tourist development council, and I was on the board, which was comprised of hoteliers, restaurateurs, and some people in the travel business like airlines, steamships, railroads, and so on. We went on missions domestically, in Canada and in Europe.

But the most important trip I made annually was to the Internationale Tourismus-Borse, known as the International

Tourism Board (ITB), in early March. It was initially six days long when it began in 1966 but has since been cut down to three. The European hoteliers would only come for a day or two but the Americans usually stayed for the entire fair. I initially went by myself to promote our Inn on the Bay hotel and Bon Appétit. After Inn on the Bay became a Best Western, they approached me to represent all of Best Westerns in Florida and offered to pay for all of my travel expenses. Since I had attended for many years already, it worked out really well for me.

ITB was, and still is, the largest global tourism event with over 250,000 attendees from over a 180 nations and territories. ITB was so large that it was held in 25 halls, as large as airplane hangars. They had city buses to take visitors from one convention hall to the other. The trade show is divided by continents and then broken down by regions. Each year, I had a booth with collateral materials in the U.S. pavilion, the most desirable of them all. Within the U.S. pavilion, we were divided by states and then by industry, for example, hotels, restaurants, cruise ships, etc. Even Disney attended for a couple of years in the beginning and then stopped. It was so large that it would be impossible to visit every booth within even a week.

The Germans are travel crazy. If they haven't had sand between their toes, they don't feel like they have been on vacation. My booth was visited by mostly Germans, some Brits, and fewer Russians. Often, while standing in my booth, I would realize that I had seen so many people that I might never see again. So, I came up with the idea of making a "tombola", a raffle. Visitors had to complete cards with their name, their address, and contact information, and place them into the tombola for a chance to win two weeks in Florida, all expenses paid. People would line up to win! The only requirement was that they had to travel within the year after attending the ITB that March.

Whenever I was in Berlin to attend ITB, I stayed at the Palace Hotel because of its convenience. At the end of the day, I would go back to the hotel with all of those completed cards and would pay one of the receptionists to type them up, and then fax the list to each of the other six Governors for the Best Western hotels in Florida. Those hotels would know when potential guests were coming to their area, how many nights they intended to stay, and what sights they hoped to visit. Generally, travelers were looking to visit the east and west coasts of Florida, up to the Orlando area at most.

The hoteliers would then follow up by contacting potential guests, giving them information about their hotel and their area, and would individually make tempting offers to stay with them, like a free extra night or free tickets to theme parks and other activities. These German people were collectors; they were thrilled to get this information along with complimentary maps highlighting all of Florida's Best Western locations. This process worked really well for many years.

I met Stan Dyck through Best Western. He was the Managing Director for all of Europe, with 1,000 hotels in 15 countries under his leadership. He was headquartered just outside of Frankfurt. During ITB week, Stan arranged and gave the party of all parties in Berlin, held at The Palace Hotel. Over 8,000 vendors in the hospitality and tourism industries were at ITB and many held parties, in every hotel, night, and supper club in and around Berlin. But Best Western gave the number one party. The word spread about Stan's parties and that's how I got to know Stan and we became good friends. People used to offer me big money to get an invitation to that party.

Another reason I stayed at the Palace Hotel? Because Sangita, their Guest Relations Manager, would always order a limousine for Stan and I, so we didn't have to take buses or taxis. You can imagine, a quarter million people going into the same area, at the same time. And I used to complain about 100 people coming for lunch at the same time at Bon Appétit!

In 1992, I met John M. at a Best Western Governor's meeting in Phoenix, Arizona. I was one of the first people to enter the cocktail reception and saw this impressive man across the room. He was good looking and could have been a model for Brooks Brothers... his tie, suit, shoes, and cuff links...I think all the way down to his underwear was Brooks Brothers. I decided that I needed to meet him. So, I went over and introduced myself to John. I told him that I liked the way he dressed and he thanked me. I asked where he had come from and he replied that he was originally from Philadelphia but had worked with Pan Am for the last 25 years. I told him that I have a lot of good friends at Pan Am. So, of course, he asked me who. I told him I knew Hans G. and his wife, Barbara, who was the country manager for Pan Am-Germany and Austria.

John later told me that after the bomb that killed 270 passengers on Pan Am Flight 103 in December of 1988 over Lockerbie, Scotland, he was responsible for keeping the victims' families updated by having meetings at 4:00 pm every day. It was an incredibly difficult job and he did it well. Pan Am never fully recovered and declared bankruptcy in January 1991, selling many of its best routes to Delta Airlines. By December of that year, Pan Am was shut down and John was out of a job. Best Western had just hired John as our Global Director of Sales and was being introduced to all of us at our Governor's meeting. I believe he had learned of the Best Western opportunity from Bill W., our Sr. VP in Sales and Marketing, who had also worked for Pan Am for many years.

That evening, John told me that he had started his Pan Am career at JFK but was then transferred to, I believe, London and then on to Berlin. He also had the opportunity to work in Japan and Australia, where he met his wife with whom he had two children. Years later they divorced, but his son still lived in Australia and his daughter moved to London.

After that meeting, John and I remained in touch and we became good friends. Because of John, Bon Appétit and Inn on the Water were able to host the Pan Am North American corporate meeting one year.

John also got to know Stan, and afterwards, we usually traveled together to attend the many industry trade shows. At ITB, we always had rooms on the same floor at the Palace Hotel. On the first night of arrival, it was always hard to fall asleep so, at 3:00 am one year, I knocked on John's door and asked him to give me a haircut. And he did.

Next to our hotel was a sauna that only the Palace Hotel guests could visit. Sangita always gave me tickets to go. I had been there several times before, but this one year, I asked John to join me. The sauna had separate changing rooms for men and women along with probably seven indoor pools and maybe 18 separate sauna rooms offering different fragrances. Outside of the changing rooms, there was a big, round bar where many naked, German women would be enjoying beer at 10:00 am in the morning.

I told John that I would meet him outside. I got undressed and headed toward the bar with my towel, however, John came out in a bathing suit. One of the women at the bar, upon seeing John, darted over like a bowing arrow, and said, "What is it with you, are you a pervert?" In Austria, bathing suits are considered unsanitary as people don't usually wash them like we do in the States. Obviously, John had to take his bathing suit off or I think that woman might have ripped it off of him. I still laugh at the memory.

Another year, I recall the publisher of an official guide that listed all of the travel companies, airlines, etc. invited some of us to a very special dinner at the Kempinski Hotel Berlin, where Stan did his apprenticeship. The private dining room was one of the sites of the Wannsee Conference of 1942. I'll never forget it. They had a large oval table that sat 50 people, not 51, but a maximum of 50. I was sitting across from a guy who was eating like an American; he cut his food, put the knife down and then changed hands to eat. I said to him, "Look behind you. See the bullet hole in the wall?" He responded, "Yes," and I said, "That was for a guy that ate just like you." The story goes that a spy in the German military had sat at that table during the Wannsee Conference. When a German soldier across from him saw him eat in this manner, he took out his gun and shot him dead at the dinner table. I then showed him where the bullet hole was still there.

In the early 90's, when London was experiencing bomb attacks from the IRA, Berlin was on high alert during ITB. My friend, Sangita in Salzburg, was married at the time to Axel, the commander of the Einsatzkommando Cobra, similar to our SWAT team. Axel happened to be off the week of ITB, so I asked him to work with me, along with his dog, which was trained for sniffing out bombs. As usual, the U.S. pavilion was the busiest so there were many undercover police officers walking around. But I had a personal bodyguard and dog guarding me; I felt very safe.

I mentioned earlier, Paula V. was one of our seven District Managers and I worked with her. She had never been to ITB, so one year I invited Paula along so she could experience the largest trade show and understand its potential to generate bookings. She was a high powered and influential person in the Best Western organization and really enjoyed the opportunity to be there. Later that week, her husband and my wife, Mary, flew in to join us. That gave me the chance to visit other pavilions with my friends, and to continue to make contacts all over the world for my future world cruise.

Rudy Münster, a German fellow, was the General Manager at The Kempinski. Back when he started, there were very few, if any, other 5-star hotels. It was shortly after WWII and Berlin was still affected by the bombings. Rudy talked his company into giving him the apartment right above the Kempinski Eck, which was a very desirable restaurant. It had all glass corners where he could people watch for hours. Rudy lived there for many years. Like me, he was a graduate of the Cornell School of Hotel Administration and had a large circle of influential guests and friends in Europe. Rudy[2] was

---

2   *London/Berlin– The Cornell Hotel Society (CHS) is awarding scholarships from the Deiv Salutskij EMEA Scholarship Fund for the Profes-*

instrumental in starting the Cornell Hotel Society of Germany and every year during ITB, he and his wife, Annelie, hosted a party for Cornell people that lived on at least three continents. It had about 120-150 members. Rudy invited me every year, and I went. After two or three years, he asked me if I had seen Annelie's new exhibition. She was a poet and a good artist. I felt obligated to buy one of her works, so I paid $3,000 for a colorful painting of a rooster that still hangs in our living room today.

Much later at ITB, after John was divorced, he met Marlene, a very attractive TV personality. He was head over heels for her and they grew close; visually they were a great fit. While at ITB that year, he also met the owners of Le Sirenuse, one of the top hotels located in Positano, Italy, and they invited him to come as their guest to the hotel. John asked if they minded if he brought friends. They didn't mind at all. So, Mary and I, John and Marlene, all flew to Milan and visited with my step-sister, Ruth, and her husband. After a few days, we rented a car and drove to Rome, where my other step-sister, Ushi, was widowed and living with her son and daughter. We spent a few days with them as well and then drove to Positano, to stay a few days at the Le Sirenuse. Afterwards, we drove to Naples and Capri, before returning to the States. Unfortunately, shortly after that trip, Marlene broke up with John and he was heartbroken.

I last attended ITB in 2016 or 2017 even though we had sold the hotel back in 2010. Like I mentioned before, I got to meet so many people and had so much fun.

The World Travel Market London, started in 1980, was also held annually in November, to help businesses attract travelers and was

---

sional Development Program (PDP), the Rudy Münster EMEA GMP Scholarship Fund for the General Managers Program (GMP) and the Leif Evensen EMEA MMH Scholarship Fund for the Master of Management in Hospitality (MMH) Program for course work on the Cornell campus in 2023. Press release, hospitalitynet.org, December 20, 2022.

attended by journalists, travel agents, tour operators, wholesalers, and for anyone that had anything to do travel. A much smaller version of ITB, with less than 500 exhibitors, it was usually attended by less than 10,000 people. While it had much less activity and structure, I attended this event, along with John M. every year as well.

We usually stayed at the Knightsbridge Hotel because it was in walking distance to the Olympia Exhibition Centre, where the convention was held. Knightsbridge is like a little village within the city and every year, John and I would go to the shoemaker to get our shoes re-soled, have our Rolexes cleaned, and to buy clothes. We also went to the Strand Theater to see all the newest plays; so it was much more relaxed.

U.S. Travel Association's IPW, commonly known as POW WOW in the travel industry, is attended by over 5,000 decision makers from global companies in the travel industry. This convention is always very upscale with wonderful accommodations and great food, and held in major cities like Los Angeles, New York, Atlanta, and Chicago. It was twice hosted in Orlando where Disney shut down the entire Magic Kingdom park for three days.

This one year, it was held in Beverly Hills, CA. Paula V. was also there, and because I had taken her to ITB in Berlin, she met many of my friends including Stan and John. So, John, Paula and I were walking around, and came to a major intersection that had been closed down in the middle of the afternoon, with cops everywhere. Every city puts their best foot forward when POW WOW visitors are in town so the city decided to host a parade of convertible cars with Hollywood actors sitting on the back, waving to everyone. I didn't recognize one single actor but everyone else seemed to be impressed.

Paula had a best friend, Marsha, who also was a District Manager with Best Western in District 3. Marsha was a country girl, who loved to fish and hunt; the total opposite of John. While watching the parade, I encouraged John to invite Marsha to Los Angeles since, as a District Manager, she would benefit from the trade show. And he did. That was the beginning of their relationship and ultimate marriage. They live in Tucson, Arizona, and I added matchmaker to my resume.

We never tried to quantify the added revenues that my attendance at these annual trade shows brought to Bon Appétit, the hotel, or to our state parks. All I can say is that I do know that we received guests from all over Europe that kept our hotel vacancies low, helped our revenues grow at Bon Appétit each year, and increased visitors to our local state parks from year to year. I'm convinced that my attendance at these trade shows for over 30 years made international travel agents aware that Florida had much to offer by way of our beautiful beaches, reasonably priced accommodations, sunny weather, and great food!

CHAPTER 19

MY ONE AND ONLY VISIT TO A LADIES' PRISON

When I joined Best Western (BW) International Hotels, corporate headquarters suggested we visit the reservation centers and do something nice for the hundreds of people that worked in them. These centers were located in Phoenix, Arizona; Tulsa, Oklahoma; and in Kansas City, Kansas. Typically, the other hotel owners that visited brought things like cookies, candy or chocolates.

I wanted to do something that people would remember us for, something special that showed more of what made our hotel different. Instead, I decided to do a cooking demonstration because 99% of the reservation center employees were women. I brought all the equipment needed, rechauds (small, portable stoves with a couple of burners to cook on) and my skillet, and food like tenderloins of beef, hollandaise sauce, choron (more like a bearnaise), etc. During their lunch hour, I stood waiting for them in my Chef's hat and jacket and would be sauteing dollar-sized tenderloin filets, placing them on toast points with some hollandaise sauce, if they wanted. It was really well received as they came back for seconds,

Above photo: Ladies' Prison in Phoenix, Arizona.

and then thirds. It was a totally different experience from what anyone else in the company had done.

We did this typically three or four times a year, and it brought wonderful results for us. When these ladies were taking reservations for a Florida stay, they usually suggested our BW Yacht Harbor Inn that had a great restaurant next door.

Later, I became aware that BW started a rehabilitation program for women who had sometimes made the wrong decisions and ended up in prison. This was an admirable concept done for the right reason to help these women. The pilot program was within a ladies' prison in Phoenix, Arizona. I thought that was an interesting challenge that I certainly wanted to take on. In this particular facility, there were about a dozen women who were able to work because they had exhibited good behavior. They answered the calls that came in on our 1-800 number, just like any other BW employee. The patrons who called to book their hotel stay had no idea they were talking to women sitting in one big prison cell.

For this visit, I brought along my partner, Karl Riedl, who wasn't as thrilled as I was for this opportunity. Typically, I brought richauds and burners with an open flame to sauté the filets. We did not have to be told that we couldn't bring equipment with open flames to a ladies' prison. I was thinking, what can we do for them, and the only thing I could come up with was to provide a large wedding cake, which we brought with us to the facility.

When we arrived at the prison, we walked to the entrance and had to ring the bell. Someone looked through a one-way glass in the door and asked what we were doing there. I replied that we were from BW, and we wanted to visit with the BW reservation center. So the guard finally opened the door and sent us to another a room where we were searched. Underneath the large cake, I had placed a large cake knife. The guard very unceremoniously ripped it out and said that we couldn't take the knife in there.

"Well," I said, "how am I supposed to cut this?"

He replied that it wasn't up for discussion. Once he had the knife, he allowed us to enter a cell where they called for escorts to take us back to the BW reservation center. Two nice-looking young ladies came across the large prison yard and approached us, saying they were there to show us to the reservation facility. The walk there was rather awkward with no conversation between us.

When we arrived, we saw about a dozen ladies sitting in one big cell with phones, computers, and brochures to help them intelligently answers the callers' questions from across the country. At the time, we had about 2,000 BW properties in North America. I didn't have a prepared presentation so I just winged it. I told them that we were so privileged to be there with them and wanted to show our appreciation for what they did and how well they did their job. I added that BW keeps track of their work and they were doing phenomenally well. As a small token of our appreciation, we had this big wedding cake for them since we could not provide them with our usual cooking demonstration. That's when I shared that Security had taken away our cake knife.

One of the ladies stood up and said, "That's not a problem" and proceeded to pull a knife out of her boots. Problem solved, and we started cutting pieces of cake for them.

As we were passing out cake, they started to warm up to us. Now we had the opportunity to have more conversation. I told them that I had never been in this type of environment before and would they mind me asking them why they were in prison.

One woman replied, "I don't know why either because I was at home cooking dinner and my husband is a fisherman. When he came home, he ran into my knife."

Soon they were all telling their stories; two women, we learned, were there for life for their involvement with Patty Hearst and the Symbionese Liberation Army crimes; another burned her house down while her husband was asleep in their home. They were hardcore criminals but they each told us that they were falsely incarcerated because it was a mistake, an accident, or whatever.

After connecting with them somewhat, I felt comfortable in sharing our mission for being there, to promote our property on the west coast of Florida, every room having a water view of the Gulf of Mexico. We had our brochures with pictures, which we left so they could share the information about us. They were impressed with our beautiful location so I extended an invitation to all of them, that when they left prison, they were welcome to come and stay with us.

"And if you like, I'll find a job for all of you," I said. I passed out my business cards to each of them, telling them they were welcome to call me anytime.

My partner, Karl, hadn't said a word yet so I introduced him, told them that he was from Bavaria and a wonderful Chef in our restaurant, which was next to the hotel. I shared that in the Best Western organization, we were known as a restaurant with rooms as compared to a hotel with a restaurant. Most BW hotels across the country were on interstates or highways, and if they had a restaurant that was operated by the ownership, they usually used the same fast-food company to provide breakfast only. We owned the only four-star restaurant with BW.

Finally, it was time to leave, and our two previous escorts were again our way out. The distance between their work facility and the entrance gate was a good walk, so we had time to talk to them this time. I asked them what brought them to prison as they were both young beautiful ladies. I don't recall their answers but I do recall them asking me if I was familiar with conjugal visits. I had no idea what that meant. They explained that I could come back and spend time alone with them, on prison property, for a weekend. I didn't understand; I was a stranger. They proceeded to explain that I could be their "cousin" and pointed to some cabins in the distance. I have to confess that I didn't ask for any further details. That time was our one and only visit to the ladies' prison in Phoenix, Arizona.

Within a couple of years, BW discontinued that program. It turned out that some of the ladies were savvy enough to share credit card numbers with family members, spouses or friends, using the business phones to go shopping for them. The theft by some resulted in the termination of the rehabilitation program for all.

CHAPTER 20

ST. LEO'S COLLEGE & ITS MONASTERY

Right from the beginning, Bon Appétit did very well. Little did we know, we were the only restaurant in town. I got to know our guests, and they appreciated what we were doing and developed relationships with them.

One day, sometime after 1985, an attorney told me he went to St. Leo's for his education. I had never heard of it. He mentioned it was in Pasco County, right next to St. Antonio, which every year has the Rattlesnake Festival. First prize at this festival goes to the person that brings the largest rattlesnake. There is also a Benedictine Monastery on the college campus. Well, of course, that got my attention since I attended Melk Abbey. So, I tried to find out how to get there and decided to visit one day.

During my visit, I walked the campus and entered the Abbey Gift Shop and Book Store. I met Brother Patrick and introduced myself. He seemed pleased to meet another Benedictine from a foreign land. He had been there for many years and ran the book store and was the face of the Monastery. Br. Patrick was very friendly

Above photo: Monastery at St. Leo's College.

and kindly gave me a tour of the Monastery. At that time, they had eight monks and a couple of postulants who are men that are thinking of becoming a monk. He invited me to a dinner that was held in a small dining room at 4:30 pm, right after Vespers (prayer time at sunset). Dinner was two slices of rye bread with a slice of cheese and tomato, with mustard and mayo available. It was wonderful!

After dinner, I asked Br. Patrick if he would be offended if one day I brought some of my people to serve dinner to the monks. He responded that I could bring anything I wanted to. And we did just that. We set up a full bar and brought a nice dinner of steaks and all the fixings. They went crazy!

As I said before, they had two postulants, one tall and thin and the other, much shorter. The tall one was particularly interested in the bar and asked our bartender for the entire bottle of the alcohol he was drinking, which I agreed to. He took the bottle, carefully placed it under his robe and kept on drinking. Mary had also attended and so I later introduced her to the tall postulant.

After the introduction, he said, "You know what? I love booze and nuns! I love nuns!" He was quite drunk and repeated it several times. The next time I visited the Abbey, he was no longer there.

I got to know the monks and went to visit them from time to time, especially when I had friends from Europe or other guests. Dating back over a hundred years ago, these monks were all alone in the orange groves. They started a little school for children and as it grew, they eventually built a priory for their Benedictine nuns. I also got to know them as well.

The former secretary to Bishop Lynch of the Diocese of St. Petersburg, Monsignor Frank Mouch, became the President of the then St. Leo College in 1987. Over the years, the school went through many transitions, and the staff of Benedictine teachers continued to shrink. Many years earlier, the Abbot had decided to give the school away to a lay board for $1.00. So the monks no longer had any responsibilities to the school but, in the contract, the school should always have a Benedictine value system. The new Board of Directors was made up of influential people, like Tom Dempsey, developer and owner of Saddlebrook Resort in Wesley Chapel, Florida, who I knew well. Most of the Board lived in Saddlebrook, and I knew many of them from my years at Innisbruck. Visiting the Abbey often, I soon met Monsignor Mouch and was asked to be on the Board. It required my attendance only once a month, so I agreed and was on the Board for about six years.

That is how I came to know Sister Germaine. She was the prioress at the priory, and I was really drawn to her because she was so nice. My willingness to be involved with the school was not about St. Leo College but about the Benedictines. While I didn't say that, they could feel it. As time went on, our Bon Appétit dinners included the nuns as well. We provided many dinners to them over the years but one Christmas in particular, I had a bus chartered to pick them all up and bring them to Bon Appétit for a private dinner on the second floor. While my mother was alive and living at the Best Western hotel, she too got to know them and liked them, and the feeling was mutual.

As I mentioned earlier, I often brought friends to the Abbey to meet the monks and Monsignor Mouch. I had a Saturday morning men's walking group. They were all of the Jewish faith so I was the token Christian. Our group was made up of Dr. Schick, a radiologist at Morton Plant Hospital, Stan Michael of Michael's Pharmacy, Larry Krug, an attorney, and Dr. Levine, a podiatrist who always walked behind Dr. Schick and would say, "Look at him, he pronates" meaning his heels got abused. It also included Manny, an investor with big bucks, and a few others. During our walks, we talked about nice things for about 10 minutes, and then the conversation went into the sewer.

In our group, we did nice things for each other. Dr. Schick, who was really nice, was head of Radiology at Morton Plant and was very successful, but he was so tight. When his birthday came around, I made arrangements with the monks to spend the weekend there. And because we were an active outdoorsy group, we drove to Saddlebrook on a Friday, parked our cars there, and then walked through orange groves for 12 miles to the monastery. I went there the day before and had dropped off an ice chest filled with fruit, sandwiches and drinks. So we were walking through the groves, and I was looking forward to a drink and a sandwich. There in the meadow, was a meeting of the Ku Klux Klan (KKK). The guys freaked out!

I told them, "Relax, relax, I got it covered." I was walking and walking, looking for the ice chest and finally found it. Some animal had broken in and ate everything so we got not a drink of water or any food.

I said, "Let me go over to those guys. I probably can get along with them and ask them for something to drink and eat."

"No, don't you dare!" was their quick reply. I reluctantly agreed and was still hungry!

So now we came to St. Leo's. I had made arrangements to stay in the Bishop's House, a nice house with three or four bedrooms. In a separate location, there was a cell for the purpose of putting up men interested in joining the order with a bed, a hanging lamp, a chair, and a sink. And that's where we put Schick. It was his birthday, and I told him, "For you, we have something special."

He responded that it was "lovely" and had everything he needed.

After we got settled, the monks invited us to Vespers, which lasted 30 minutes. It is an honor to attend, to be seated up front among the monks. We watched as they sang and prayed. Schick was next to me, and when it came to kneeling, we all knelt except Schick. He remained standing while everyone else was on their knees.

I whispered to him, "Schick, down," but he said no. All the monks were looking at him because he stood out like a sore thumb and was being disrespectful.

I repeated again, "Get down" and again he said, "No, Jews don't kneel."

I responded, "Yes, but Benedictines do, and you're in their house now, so get down." He wouldn't. When Vespers was over, we went to dinner. We sat in the same place I had been before and again served two slices bread, mustard, mayonnaise, cheese and tomato was for dinner.

After dinner, Schick asked me where the closest city or town was. He wanted to get something for the room. The monk responded that it was nearly eight miles away.

So, Schick said, "Can you ask your friends if we can borrow a car?"

And one monk who was sitting at our table turned to the Abbot and said, "Let him walk. He won't kneel."

But anyway, I got the car, and we drove to the town. What did he want? Manischewitz wine and food. We took it back to the Bishop's House because it was the end of their day. We stayed up until 2:00 or 3:00 in the morning all together, with some of my monk friends that had joined us. We had wonderful conversations, and we really connected. Friendships were built that night.

One of my friends was Br. Bennett, an Italian who barely spoke any English. He liked my mother, and she liked him, so I would pick him up sometimes, bring him to dinner with my mother, and then drive him home. One day, I went to visit with him, and we went to walk by Lake Jovita behind the monastery and school campus. While we walked, I asked questions but he didn't talk much. He was kind but reserved because he didn't speak much English.

We continued to walk, and I said, "Brother Bennett, how long have you been here?"

He didn't answer, so we continued to walk and walk. Finally, he said, "Thirrrrrrrrrty yeaaaaaaaars."

I responded, "Oh my goodness, that's a long time." We walked and we walked, and we saw the cemetery.

Out of the blue, he said, "Forrrrrrrrrrrty yeaaaaaaaaars." He didn't know how long he had been there; he had lost a decade.

Upon arriving at the cemetery, I mentioned that it was a special place. He replied, "Yes, one day I will be here. Will you come and visit me?" I asked him if he wanted me to. He said yes. I have kept my promise and have visited his grave many times.

CHAPTER 21

RELATIONSHIP WITH THE STATE OF FLORIDA

Shortly after we opened Bon Appétit, probably within the first two years or so, I got a visit from representatives from Tallahassee with the Florida State Park Division. They wanted me to consider helping them with some issues they had with transportation and food service on Caladesi Island.

As a side note, at that time, Bon Appétit was closed on Wednesdays, so we often held a BBQ for the staff and their families on Caledesi. They had a large observation tower that was enjoyable to climb so we were familiar with the island and its beautiful beach.

They explained that they had a building that included a food concession and a contract with an individual that provided transportation to the island that was not working well. They had a boat, of sorts, that ran out of the marina next to Bon Appétit. People would park at the marina and then board the boat to Caladesi Island and returned later that day. They were supposed to offer this service daily, but at least two or three times a week, the boat would not be

Above photo: Wedding pavilion on Honeymoon Island, Dunedin, Florida.

working or was out of gas, and people got stuck on the boat. People were complaining heavily, writing letters to Tallahassee about the poor service. The department was experiencing a lot of heat, and they finally decided to make a change.

First, they were no longer using the current concession operator and were looking for someone to provide food and beverages on the island like hot dogs, hamburgers, and snacks, along with beverages like water and sodas. They also offered beach chair rentals.

I listened and then in earnest, asked how I would bring the food over and the employees and any other provisions needed to the island.

"Well, you'd probably have to get a boat," he replied.

Then I asked about the ferry that transported visitors. He responded that they would advertise for interested parties to send them a Request for Proposal (RFP) to provide the transportation. At the end of the meeting, I told them that we would be very happy to try and help, for them and the community. They were really thrilled and couldn't have been nicer.

I had never been in St. Joseph's Sound Bay and had no idea of how deep it was. I asked if they had any recommendations for a boat. They said that there were many shallow spots near Bon Appétit so they recommended we purchase a mullet boat. Not knowing what a mullet boat was, they explained that it was a fiberglass boat that has the engine up front along with the steering station. It could go into water only a couple of inches deep and as you gain speed, the front lifts and the engine won't get grounded.

They referred me to a boat builder in Maitland, Florida on U.S. 19 who built the "Cadillac" of mullet boats.

Long story short, we purchased one, which by the way, was good looking and fun to drive. Then we hired two sisters who we took out to Caladesi Island every morning along with food and provisions, and then picked them up at the end of the day. They did a good job for eight or nine years.

The owner of the Starlite dinner boat, Phil H, along with his wife, won the RFP for the concession on the ferry to Caladesi Island. It all worked fine for many years although for those first eight to nine years, we didn't make a penny but, we continued to provide the service because we liked the relationship and the people in the State Parks Division. The wooden structure housing our concession on Caladesi was nice but over the years, we updated the equipment and added walk-in coolers. It has a beautiful marina with floating docks that remains the same to this day.

We met with the Tallahassee team usually once a year. One year, they said, "We know you are honest."

I asked, "How do you know that?"

They responded that they have 175 state parks and, on average, across the state, they get 91 or 92 cents per visitor. But our group sent more than that.

That's when I responded, "Yeah, that's why I didn't take a salary!" As a result, they asked if we would be interested in taking over Honeymoon Island as well. I was not very familiar with Honeymoon Island but guessed it offered a different experience for visitors.

I was agreeable to considering it but wanted to know how they were running it then. They had a park manager and park rangers, who all carried guns as law enforcement on Honeymoon Island. Unfortunately, the park manager was having an inappropriate relationship with his secretary and was known to pull his gun on visitors.

They had four identical buildings in close proximity to each other on the north side of the island. They were solidly built to sustain high winds of 250 miles per hour. They were all being used as restroom facilities, each having one restroom for males and one for females. We were allowed to relocate two of the buildings, which we did. They were moved to the southern part of the island, closer to the entrance gate.

One building was repurposed to house what is now known as the Café, with cooking equipment and refrigeration. The other side of the building we left as restrooms, dividing them into smaller facilities. The rangers were responsible for sanitation and maintenance of the restrooms. Afterwards, we added merchandise to the Café that included towels, swimming gear, etc. in addition to food and beverages.

When we took Honeymoon Island over, I believe they had about 325,000 visitors a year. After a couple of years of success, the State came back to us and asked, "Peter, what can you think of to increase visitation and more entry revenue?"

At that time, it was $5.00 per car, and now it's $8.00 per vehicle. I gave it some thought, and replied, "Well, its name is Honeymoon Island, so it implies weddings." I shared that we would build a wedding pavilion. They liked the idea and then asked if we would participate financially in building this pavilion. Since it was my idea, I said sure, as long as our contract period was long enough to recover our investment.

We agreed, and they agreed. We used a local architect to draw up the plans with a cost, at that time of $500,000. Unfortunately, it took 10 years from that meeting to sign the contract to build the pavilion because turnover in Tallahassee-based government officials kept postponing our progress. In the meantime, we helped make weddings happen on Honeymoon Island with chair rentals, décor, and catering.

During those 10 years, a lot of the beach was lost, and the two northern buildings were now over water. They moved one to a new location which is now the Museum and Visitor Center, and the other was moved further east, towards the parking lot and away from the water.

Once we could go ahead with actually building the pavilion, the cost had more than doubled to nearly $1.2 million dollars. Because Tallahassee has prolonged the construction, we agreed to pay $700,000 with the remaining paid by the State. Once construction started, it took 18 months to complete. On September 11, 2001, I attended a meeting in Orlando with the State and all the concessionaires. The meeting started at 8:00 am, and the officials proceeded to explain that we had to pay for the "privilege" of running our business at the state parks. Everyone's contracts were negotiated independently, and they claimed to be our business partners. (I was thinking, yeah, you take the money, and we do the work.) Anyway, they came to me and asked how I wanted to continue to do business with them. At that time, it was customary to pay 10% of gross sales, and I agreed that it was fair to do so.

Here in Florida, we have mostly sunshine, but we do have rainy days, hurricanes, and red tide, which account for enough days in a year that it makes a difference. On those days that we're closed, we owe nothing to them and have no expenses either. Over the years, expenses have increased by way of our electricity use, based on guesses as they don't have meters. But the charges are not enough to make a difference to our bottom line.

During that meeting, the State also mentioned that they had signed a contract with a developer, giving them exclusive rights to build bungalows in any of the state parks. And for that privilege, they would pay 15% of gross revenues. The rest of us would gradually move up to 15% with future contract renewals (as of 2021, we pay the state 15%, and with 1,600,000 visitors to the parks, Honeymoon Island and Caladesi Island combined, they are very happy with us). No one was happy with the increase from 10 to 15%. Before discussions could continue, someone interrupted the meeting to say that we needed to watch the television. The first terrorist plane had hit the Twin Towers in New York City.

I decided to stay that night in Orlando and met with management. We had dinner, and I brought up the deal with the developer. He had attended the meeting, and to me, he looked like a gangster, and as it turned out, he was. I was confused as to why they would bring some other developer in. On Honeymoon Island, I would have loved to build bungalows as we had a demand for it. I was the one that had given them the idea to increase visitors by marketing weddings on the beach. They replied that they couldn't go back on their executed contract. Some phone discussions continued afterwards without much progress.

During those 10 years, the Assistant Director and I communicated well. I would visit Tallahassee periodically. He called me one day and said, "You know, Peter, you made some comments that we made a mistake with that developer."

I said, "Yes, well I thought so, but you know better. You're my boss, so to speak." He said they had a problem with this developer. The first project was in an Orlando state park where they had paid $5 million just to build a road to where cabins were to be built. The firm was not performing according to the contract.

A little background is needed here. Before this conversation with the Assistant Director, the developer had already called me. He had been told by the State to call me because Honeymoon Island was the perfect place to build bungalows, right on the beach. So, he came to visit, and I showed him Honeymoon Island. Long story short, the developer told me that he would give me the opportunity to invest $250,000, and we would go from park to park and collect the money up front. We would never actually build the cabins, but instead, he suggested, that we sell those contracts to Marriott. That's when I knew he was a crook.

So, back to my call with the Assistant Director. When I recounted my visit and discussions with the developer, he didn't like it at all. He got the State's Attorney General involved who then called me. They invited me to Tallahassee or they would subpoena me.

I replied that I would be glad to come to Tallahassee since I had been there many times, and I liked everyone there. He asked me more detailed questions about my conversation with the developer and set up an appointment. He also mentioned that they would call me as a witness. Because of turnover at the State level, it was a couple of years before there was a trial. During the trial, the judge asked me to recount my conversations with the developer, and how I didn't feel right about it and, as a result, did not move forward with it. I added that the developer had no intentions of building the bungalows. The developer's attorney stood up, vehemently objecting to my statement, asking how could I know his client's intentions.

The judge looked at me, and I replied, "Because he told me so. He intended to sell the contracts to Marriott."

That was it, and I was told I could leave, and the developer's contracts were canceled by the State. I heard later that the developer sued the State for a huge amount, was awarded an undisclosed lesser amount, but never built a single bungalow.

CHAPTER 22
HILLBOROUGH RIVER STATE PARK

Since this time, to make any major improvements or additions to state parks, the State has a procedure that they have to follow when they go into a community. They held a public meeting in Dunedin at my request at the Senior Center on Douglas Street. It was attended by a representative from Tallahassee, lawyers, rangers, and other appropriate management. I still wanted to build bungalows on Honeymoon Island and had to share the plans, why and how.

There was a large turnout, with most residents from Royal Stewart Arms condominiums, which is in walking distance to the park's entrance. They were vehemently against it, with no exception; not one person spoke up for the project except for myself. Their greatest concern was increased traffic and that people would be staying in the park overnight which may lead to crime. We tried again five years later with the same outcome. I decided not to go there again, especially since many of those residents were guests of Bon Appétit, and I didn't want to be confrontational with them.

Once the pavilion was completed, we advertised with billboards on U.S. 19, added a website and marketed it through Bon Appétit. Before long, we were handling hundreds of wedding ceremonies a year, some with receptions on the island while others decided on more formal receptions at Bon Appétit. With about five miles of beach, some of the coastline is rocky and not conducive to holding weddings. Sand was brought in to create large enough areas that are numbered. All weddings must be permitted to ensure the area is available, cordoned off, and set-up with chairs and décor to make the wedding venue as comfortable and as beautiful as possible.

Because of our long relationship in good standing with the State, we were made aware of the Request for Proposal (RFP) for concessions on Sand Key, and we applied. When we won the contract, with our experience on Honeymoon Island, we felt that we would be successful on Sand Key as well.

One weekend, not that long ago, I drove down to Sand Key and personally witnessed eight weddings being held simultaneously. With their officiants, couples were waiting for their vows to be exchanged at the setting of the sun on the horizon.

The State has put us on a pedestal as to how we handled our financials. As concessionaires we used to have annual meetings with state park officials, and they often suggested to other concessionaires that they should handle financial reporting and pay fees to the State like we did. Since 2021, the State requires we now send in our monthly revenue reports, which get reviewed by one department and, if approved, we then send in our 15% fees. Once received by the State, two more departments review the information for accuracy.

I was on vacation in Europe when my partner, Karl, received a call from the State of Florida to take over Hillsborough River State Park that had been managed by State employees. The State built a $1 million swimming pool and was not able to turn a profit. Upon my return, the Assistant Director in Tallahassee, Mr. R. called me.

We had worked together for many years by then, and we got along very well. He asked me if we could take over the Hillsborough River State Park, and I replied, send me your financial statements.

When he did, we could not interpret them at all, they were so confusing. So, I called him back and told him that, according to their financial statements, we could not move forward. He offered to restructure the financials and send them back to us. Again, after reviewing them, our answer was the same. We really wanted to help but it didn't make sense. First of all, the park was an hour and half away from Dunedin, so it would be a three-hour round-trip for our employees, not including the hours of operation. It just wasn't economical for us.

One night soon after, Mr. R. called me at home. He said, "Peter, you have to take it on, because if not, we will all get fired here. The governor said, 'Get this project organized, we just spent an extra $1 million for a swimming pool, and you can't make it work.' So, you have to help us."

"Well, okay, let me think about how we can do that," I replied.

He said that I didn't have to think about it, he just needed a yes or no answer. He wasn't threatening, just desperate. Whatever or however we wanted to structure it was fine, we just had to take it over.

That is when I replied, "Mr. R, I don't want to embarrass you or shock you or take advantage of anything, but I could offer only a small percentage of our revenue."

I suggested this small amount, hoping he would turn me down, but his answer was, "You got it! We'll send you the contract, sign it."

So, we took it over. All of the State employees left except the manager who lived in Dade City. She would close the park at the end of the day, and on the way home, she was supposed to deposit the day's revenue into the night depository at Sun Bank, also in Dade City. We changed the menus and put in place the same procedures that worked at the other parks. Nothing seemed to work right for whatever reason. We weren't making revenue, and so I met with our Controller and asked him when was the last time he had checked on their deposits. He said they were being made daily as was reflected in the financials. He pulled them up and as he looked, he realized they were missing. He thought it was a mistake.

I decided to drive to the Sun Bank in Dade City, which is a small community of several mobile home parks where everyone knows one another. That is one of the reasons the State decided to build a swimming pool since most living there did not have access to that type of recreation. I spoke to the Branch Manager who said they had not seen the park manager or deposits in weeks.

I had no choice but to call the police and file a report. They investigated and learned that instead of depositing the funds into the bank, she was betting them at the casino every night. They arrested her, but her husband agreed to a payment plan for restitution of the thousands of dollars stolen from us. We ran the Hillsborough River State Park for six years without a profit. We did not renew the contract but stayed there until they found a replacement concessionaire that also ran another park. The initial contract was for five years, and I heard he did not renew either.

Back in 2011, soon after Rick Scott became the Governor of Florida, I received a call that he was going to visit the Hillsborough River State Park the next day, and they requested that I welcome him. I agreed and arrived at the gatehouse at 8:00 am the next morning where all our employees were waiting as well. I saw a group of people standing off to the side.

I said to one of the ladies, "I understand the big boss is coming today."

She didn't answer but then I saw a guy come out from behind her in a ranger uniform, and he said, "I'm the big boss."

Quickly I replied, "Well, welcome!" He noticed I had an accent and asked where I came from. I told him that I was from Vienna, Austria, and he said his wife loved Vienna. I asked him to stay for lunch in our café, and he did. I introduced him to our manager and all the employees, and we had wonderful conversation for the next two hours.

In the 1980s, I was commuting back and forth to teach a couple of courses for a semester at The Cornell School of Hotel Administration. I usually flew up on Wednesday afternoons to Ithaca, would have a standing date for dinner with a former professor of mine, and then flew home on Friday evenings. One week, it was Hotel Ezra Cornell[3], a big annual event in the Hotel School, so I decided to stay for the weekend. Mary flew up, and I showed her around the campus, my office, and the classrooms where I taught. We were attending an arranged dinner and took a bus to the Hotel Ezra Cornell event. The bus was filled with hotel students and graduates and most knew one another.

We got on the bus and then I heard this deep voice, "Peter, Peter, I've been looking for you all day. Where have you been?" I replied that I had been in my office all day.

---

3 *Hotel Ezra Cornell (HEC) is a three-day, student-run business conference for hospitality industry leaders and members of the Cornell community from across the globe. A 97-year tradition of the School of the Hotel Administration, HEC is one of the oldest organizations at Cornell and an unparalleled introduction to the students, faculty, and alumni of the preeminent hospitality program in the nation. Featuring some of the most talented individuals in the business, the conference will discuss the latest developments in hospitality and include leisure events for attendees to network with other professionals and meet the students who will be leading the industry in the future. [Cornell website]*

Peter B introduced me to his wife, and I introduced Mary to them.

I said, "Peter, I hear you are a millionaire" to which his wife responded, "Billionaire." He asked when I had arrived and when we would be going back. Talking rather loudly, he told us that we needed to fly back with them in his Lear jet. The next day, Peter took us to the airport and gave us a tour of his plane, we met his co-pilot, and he asked when we wanted to leave. I told him that I really appreciated his offer but we already had return tickets and that I was a little claustrophobic.

It turned out that Rick Scott also got along very well with Peter B, a former Cornell classmate of mine, and visited him in Destin, Florida. At that time, there was no good connector road to and from Destin to Interstate 10. Peter B, the Governor, and I had a wonderful meal and conversation. At the end, Governor Scott asked if there was anything that Peter needed and he replied, "Yes, you can build us a connector from I-10." He asked about the cost, which I don't recall, but I do remember that the Governor said, "You got it."[4]

Peter B was, of course, a big financial supporter of Governor Scott. Along with seven other Scott supporters, they were placed on a committee to study the needs of Florida and made recommendations to the Governor.

---

4   *US 331 was started in December 2013 and finally was completed three years later in mid-2017. This two-lane road cost $118.5 million (Wikipedia)*

CHAPTER 23

BON APPÉTIT TRAVEL AGENCIES

During the 47 years of owning Bon Appétit, we also started three travel agencies. Two of them were regular travel agencies geared towards European travel. We had licensed and qualified people running those agencies. Having the hotel and restaurant, mostly local people shared that they really enjoyed what we were doing and approached us to put together trips that were a little bit more intimate. So, we started a niche travel agency for friends and guests who wanted me to lead tours of Europe. Our trips were mostly to Austria and Germany.

During one to trip to Salzburg and Southern Germany, I took our group to the Kehlsteinhaus (known in English as the Eagle's Nest), which is a building that was constructed by the Nazis, atop the summit of the Kehlstein that rises above the Obersalzberg in southeast Germany. It used to be known at Hitler's Tea House, but after the atrocities of World War II, that name was no longer permitted. And Hitler hated it because he had terrible panic attacks from his fear of heights. And in that sense, I can identify, because

Above photo: Porsche trip visit to Swarovski headquarters in Tyrol, Austria.

I hate heights as well. To get to the top, we took a bus up winding roads. I mean, it was a frightful experience for me. And then, when the bus could go no further, they used vans to take us up the next leg until we reached an elevator for the remaining 86 flights, built before the Second World War. I didn't want to go in an elevator that was over a 100 years old. Fortunately, there was an attendant in there and the rest of the group convinced me to go with them. It easily held 20 people and was beautifully decorated with brass inside.

This building was commissioned by Hitler's officers because they believed he was going to be the leader of the free world. They hosted Heads of States from other countries that he had occupied or "annexed," according to Hitler. It was meant to be impressive to other leaders, but Hitler still hated it.

I have a friend, Peter S, also from Austria. He lives here locally and owns Fast Lane Travel (which celebrates its 50th anniversary in 2024). He puts together European trips, mostly with guests driving Porsches. In Austria, the first Volkswagen was built. Between the First World War and the Second World War, there was a long period of starvation and extreme poverty. So Hitler came up with the idea to build autobahns, those now-famous highways in Europe. And in order to utilize these highways, he more or less commissioned Dr. Ferdinand Porsche, an Austrian engineer. The first car Dr. Porsche built was the first Volkswagen (VW) that means "the people's car," because it was very reliable, solidly built and economical. Almost everyone could afford it.

Dr. Porsche also designed and manufactured the Porsche sports car. They are manufactured in Stuttgart, Germany and are one of the major employers there. Porsches are considered a very popular brand in the United States because they are well designed and very reliable. In this country, you can legally drive only 70 miles an hour whereas Porsches can easily go much faster than that. So Peter S, who loves the Porsche and is a car fanatic, organizes Porsche tours back to the old country, where it was designed and built. Peter started promoting these tours, and they have become very successful, so much so, that he asked me if I would consider taking a group to Europe. Some already drove Porsches in America and some ordered Porsches from Germany and took delivery to spend a few weeks or a month driving it around Europe before having it shipped to the United States. And finally, others take this tour for the experience to lease and drive through Europe in a fancy fast car.

I led a group of 48 people in 24 Porsches from September 27th to October 8th in 2000. My driver was Joerg, the chief engineer for Porsche in Germany. We flew into Stuttgart and were then taken to the factory to pick up our Porsches. We drove through the Black Forest on our way to Bodensee, a small town on Lake Constance, the second largest lake in Austria. We checked into a beautiful hotel right on the lake with lots of parking. One of the reasons we stayed there was because, with 24 Porsches, we needed a lot of space to ensure these cars didn't bang into one another. Everyone went up to their hotel rooms, changed and came down for a dinner cruise on Lake Constance. We had music along with a candlelit dinner including white glove service.

The next morning, I told everyone at breakfast that we were going from Germany through Austria and told them to be mindful of the speed limits. In Germany, they could drive as fast as they wanted on the autobahn, but in Austria, it's 130 kilometers per hour, which is about 80 miles per hour and significantly slower. I gave them detailed maps with instructions for each day of the trip but they could make stops or side trips as they pleased. I also gave each couple a booklet of questions, with pictures, to be answered along their chosen routes. For example, on one page next to a picture was the question, "In which little village did you see this church?" Correct answers were given so many points, and at the end of the trip, the couple with the most points won a prize.

Before we left, I mentioned, "Whoever gets the most expensive speeding ticket will get first prize. So, here we go." We left Germany, entered into a long tunnel that brought us into Austria. And there we met "Gendarmerie", local police officers and their sign that said, STOP. They had clocked us coming through the tunnel, way over the speed limit.

I was in the first car, and there were 23 cars behind us. I had kept reminding my stubborn German driver, Joerg, to slow down, to 130 kilometers. The Austrian police don't have a sense of humor so I told Joerg to let me talk to them and to not say anything. I walked up to the officer who saluted me with a big smile on his face (he saw me as a fat paycheck).

Meanwhile, Joerg rolled down his window and started yelling at the officer. I said, "Officer, don't listen to him. He's from Germany." He asked me where was I from, and I told him Vienna, Austria.

He then replied, "You have a little American accent."

I responded that I lived in America now. That's when the officer told me that his radar gun came from America.

I said, "Really? Do you mind if I look through it?"

He said he didn't mind at all and while I was looking through his radar gun, I saw two of our Porsches speed through. Then, I clocked a white Jaguar with Swiss plates and quickly informed the officer that they were speeding and that he needed to stop them, which he did. And as he wrote that driver a speeding ticket, the remaining 21 Porsches went through without being stopped.

We continued through the Alps and stopped at another lake in Austria, where we met for lunch in a castle. After lunch, I had them show me any speeding tickets received. The winner was a $180 ticket.

We then went from there to Saalfelden, where next door, was an Austrian AAA equivalent facility, where we could drive our cars at any speed. It is a big arena where visitors can learn to maneuver their cars on a track that can change surfaces quickly, from bone dry to black ice. It is a special track, but they have several of them in Austria, so people can learn to adjust to various weather conditions.

After the race track, I took them to the Swarovski headquarters where the crystals are cut into jewelry and figurines. We visited the museum and their shop inside so everyone had an opportunity to buy jewelry and gifts. Swarovski is open 363 days a year and closed for only two days a year for maintenance. Later that night, we ate, drank and danced the night away.

The highest mountain in Austria is Grossglockner, and we drove up the High Alpine Road. Joerg told me that he was going to show me how to drive up without ever using the brakes. And he did going up, which was no big deal.

On the way up, I noticed a number of tractors on the side of the road. I asked Joerg what the tractors were doing there. He said they were there because sometimes cars overheated, especially from using the brakes so much on the way down. True to his word, he never touched the brake but constantly downshifted the whole way down the mountain.

We then stayed outside of Salzburg where I took the group on a *Sound of Music* tour and theater show, pointed out the beautiful Baroque architecture of Salzburg, went to the Museum of Marionettes, and ordered Salzburger Nockerl for everyone to taste... a dessert that is as sweet as a dream and as tender as a kiss. It is my favorite dessert, unfortunately, not available in the U.S.

After a couple of nights in Vienna, we returned to Stuttgart to drop off the cars at Porsche. The factory closes at noon. There's a loud siren, and everyone drops what they were doing and leaves for a huge dining room that probably seats over 1,000 people. From the most junior mechanic apprentice to the Chairman of the Board, everybody eats lunch at the same time and in the same place. We were invited to lunch with them and afterwards, they took all of us on a test drive. We had professional drivers, and they were going so fast, that some of my tour group were not feeling well afterwards. They were petrified and will never forget their experience.

The opportunity to put these trips together came to us. So many of Bon Appétit guests over the years wanted to see Europe through European eyes. I knew we needed at least 16 people to 20 people to go because even 23 years ago, 5-star hotels were expensive and we were able to get them at greatly discounted rates. Otherwise, no one could have afforded this trip. Hosting these guided tours came with great responsibility that I took very seriously.

CHAPTER 24

HONORING THE QUIET PROFESSIONALS

The core of my success has always been in my strong belief in service to others. That belief led to my involvement in local community events and participating on different Boards like the Clearwater and Dunedin Chambers of Commerce and with Morton Plant Hospital.

It is this involvement that led me to attending a simulated airplane hijacking at the Clearwater Chamber of Commerce meeting in the early 1990's. The doors suddenly burst open and camouflaged men invaded into the dining room. One of them threw a grenade to the front of the room. It was caught by Richard "Dick" Leandri, who reinserted the pin just in the nick of time. Dick was a loyal supporter of the US Army Rangers and served as the event facilitator that day. I learned about the intense preparation and training that is undertaken by our military personnel. I was so impressed! It also was the start of a friendship between Dick and me.

As a result of my keen interest, Dick invited me to accompany him on a road-trip to Fort Benning, Georgia to attend the Army's

Above photo: SOCOM Memorial at MacDill AFB.

annual "Best Ranger" competition. While on this eight-hour trip, Dick told me about his civilian armada, the Chairborne Rangers. It is a non-military organization that funded the design and construction of the US Army Ranger Memorial located at Fort Benning.

On the drive back, Dick also told me about his failing health and asked me to do him a favor. I recall him saying, "Peter, I want you to do for the Special Operations Command at MacDill what I have done for the US Army Rangers in Fort Benning."

I never had any military experience and barely knew the difference between the responsibilities of the Army and Navy. Yet, I was very intrigued and Dick promised to help, so together we decided to make it happen.

Our first step was to meet with four-star General Wayne Downing, Commander-in-Chief of the Special Operation Command (SOCOM) at MacDill Air Force Base in Tampa. General Downing, I learned, loved to jump out of perfectly good airplanes as a hobby. He told us that active military personnel could not serve on this project. Only civilians and retired military could participate in creating a Special Operations Memorial. With Dick's help, we recruited a civilian team with retirees Major General Joseph Lutz and Geoff Barker, and began to ask for donations to this worthy cause.

I was nominated to be the first President of the SOCOM Foundation with a greater challenge than I had expected. Our list of potential donors had never heard of SOCOM and that was understandable. These military personnel operated in highly secretive circumstances, not able to tell their family and friends anything about their missions or where they were going at a moments' notice. They were "the quiet professionals." They would leave MacDill quickly to whatever secret destination was assigned, complete their mission and then return home without a word to anyone.

Dick and I were committed to this project. It took several years of knocking on doors to raise all the money needed before the memorial could be designed and built. Finally, the memorial foundation received approval from Bill Clinton's Secretary of the Air Force, Sheila Widnall, and the first SOCOM Memorial was built at MacDill Air Force Base (AFB). The original memorial was a wall, inscribed with 137 names, of Special Operations personnel who had made the ultimate sacrifice in training or in action.

Our Foundation continued to meet after the Memorial was built in 1999. We continued to raise funds to cover ceremonies and events, maintenance, and new plaques as they were added. In 2006, a local businessman was being shown around MacDill AFB and stopped at the SOCOM memorial. He was so touched by the memorial that he got in touch with our Foundation and offered to provide the construction of an expansion, at his cost. After the 9/11 terrorist attacks and the deployment of thousands of troops to Iraq, we had a lot of names to add. The second memorial, an exterior wall, was built and open to the public in 26 days after its groundbreaking. The back of the surrounding wall honors the donors who made this memorial possible.

CHAPTER 25

JOINT CIVILIAN ORIENTATION CONFERENCE

As one of the founders, and the first Chairman and President of the Special Operations Memorial Foundation, I was given the rare opportunity to attend a Joint Civilian Orientation Conference (JCOC).

We intentionally picked certain civilians that never served in the military but who were willing to serve on this Foundation's Board. Its purpose was to gather the funds to create and build a memorial located at MacDill Air Force Base in Tampa, Florida to bring about awareness of what Special Operations has done. The idea originated in the Pentagon, with the first Secretary of Defense, James V. Forrestal, under President Truman. His thoughts were that many citizens who never served in the military did not like what the military did. So he started this program, the JCOC. He felt there were known troublemakers, mostly in academia, i.e., college presidents, provosts, etc. Of course, there were others who were strong supporters of the military.

Above photo: Handing a $2,000 check to the Air Force Base Commander.

The 59th Annual JCOC was held from April 22-28, 1996. This program was managed through the Pentagon. Coincidentally, on this particular trip that lasted a week, Linda Tripp headed up this conference. She also had an important role in the vetting and selection process of the people to invite. To create the list, she asked the various commanders of U.S. military bases to send recommendations. There were 15 people from each service branch; Army, Navy, Air Force, and Marine Corps, for a total of 60 people. Each team, by service branch, had one cadre to keep us on point and out of trouble. With each invitation, there were obligations. Linda, with her assistant, Monica Lewinsky (who had worked with her previously in the White House), put this conference together.

Some of the attendees were the Mayor of Orlando, the Secretary of State from Connecticut, the Principal Deputy Assistant Secretary of Defense for Public Affairs, and many other governmental officials. Each service branch attendee was assigned a specific color for the duration of the conference. Army wore green, Navy wore dark blue, Air Force wore light blue, and Marine Corp wore red. I was recommended by Four Star General Peter J. Schoomaker, Commander of Special Operations at MacDill AFB, and therefore, I wore light blue.

To begin our week of JCOC, we met on Monday night at the Ritz-Carlton Washington, D.C. in the West End, near downtown. Introductions were made, and several dignitaries spoke. One of the speakers was Samuel ("Sandy") Berger, who at the time was serving as the Deputy National Security Advisor for the Clinton Administration. We were also each given a large binder that included a brief bio on each participant, in alphabetical order, and by which service branch we were under.

After the speakers, we had a dinner that was very formal with many protocols. During dinner, the military bands of each service branch played. Admiral Jeremy "Mike" Boorda also attended the dinner; he was known as a "Sailor's Sailor," a "Mustang," the first enlisted sailor to rise continuously from the ranks to become Chief of Naval Operations. I thought him an incredible guy with unbelievable accomplishments. Sadly, about two weeks later, in May 1996, he committed suicide[5] by a self-inflicted gunshot wound to the heart, wearing his uniform and all of his medals.

The Secretary of the Navy made the first presentation, and I recall them saying that wherever there is a trouble spot in the world, they were the first responders as they steam across the ocean and bring the Marines with them. The Army added that they march into trouble.

Dr. Widnall was the last to speak and said, "The United States certainly has the most superior Navy; there's no debate about what the Army can do, but when you really need to get there quickly, you call 911, the Air Force." The Air Force can get to anywhere in the world within six hours, usually flying a B-2 Bomber or C-17 Night Hawk from Nevada.

On Tuesday morning, we had breakfast and met with Service Secretaries, the Chairman of the Joint Chiefs of Staff, and other senior Department officials. We also had the opportunity to visit the National Military Command Center to learn how military activities were monitored around the world. What we received was an overview of defense and national security issues, and how they impacted each of the services. That afternoon, we left from

---

5 *Boorda died by suicide by shooting himself in the chest after leaving suicide notes reported to contain expressions of concern that he had tarnished the reputation of the Navy, following a media investigation into the legitimacy of his having worn on his uniform two service ribbons with bronze "V" devices, which indicate the awards were for acts of valor. The "V" devices are by regulation only to be awarded to personnel who performed an act of valor in actual combat, and Boorda had not served in combat. Boorda had removed the two ribbon devices on his uniform almost a year before he died and was generally perceived as having made a good-faith error in believing he was authorized to wear the devices. [Wikipedia]*

Andrews Air Force Base aboard a C-17 Globe Master which can transport tanks, bombs, troops, or anything else needed for war. They are still used today. All of us were seated along with our luggage. I was seated next to the Postmaster General. Actually, we were seated back-to-back, so I turned around to introduce myself.

He said his name was P.T. so I asked him, "Any relationship to Andy T.?"

He said that was his nephew. I responded that Andy had been a classmate of mine at Cornell. And he responded, "And your point is?"

I wasn't sure how to respond so I just said, "Just checking," and turned around.

During the flight, we were able to move around, visit the cockpit, and get to know one another better. We arrived in Norfolk, Virginia where the base commanders made presentations to us. We were then escorted onto an aircraft carrier pier side, where we had cocktails and hors d'oeuvres on the deck while we were presented with interesting facts about the ship.

On Wednesday, our third day, we were flown in a C-2 "Greyhound," a fixed wing, propeller-driven aircraft onto the deck of the Navy's nuclear-powered aircraft carrier, the USS Theodore Roosevelt. We entered this C-2 plane from the back where our seats were facing the rear so the pilots were to our backs, and we had no windows. We were not only strapped in across our chests, but we also had to wear a crash helmet, a life vest (with lights and whistles), and goggles.

While we were onboard, we were able to observe the launch and recovery of tactical aircraft, learn about flight operations, the role of the carrier battle group, and see how thousands of sailors live and work aboard their "floating city." We were also shown the warships that go along and surround the aircraft carrier. They have missiles and, if anyone comes close or flies over, they don't ask questions, they just shoot. There are typically 5,000 people on a carrier along with all the aircraft that must be protected. After a short flight, we had the opportunity to experience an "arrested" landing whereby the hook on the plane connects to one of four cables on the aircraft carrier. A perfect landing is hooking cable number three from 120 mph to a stop in two seconds.

I was sitting next to a preacher on this flight and before we landed, I recall that I said to him, "Now is the time to pray." Naturally, we had an expert pilot who caught cable three with ease.

When we were taken to the control tower on the aircraft carrier, the commander said, "Look at Johnny here. He's not even 18 years old, and he drove the aircraft carrier with a joystick on the bridge. Don't let anybody tell you that young people are no good in America anymore."

A lady in our group then said to the commander that she was sorry to tell him, but she just couldn't go back to shore on the C-2 again. He responded, "No problem, come with us for the next six months. Be our guest and stay with us until we arrive at the harbor." I think they gave her some medicine to help because she was on our flight back. I kind of understood how she felt as the plane looked like a flying sewing machine.

After lunch, we got to experience a catapult-assisted takeoff from the carrier and were flown back ashore to Norfolk for port tours of a nuclear-powered attack submarine, the USS Hyman G. Rickover,[6] as well as a surface combatant, to complete our day with the Navy.

I was very concerned about the tour of the submarine as I am claustrophobic. Anyway, to descend into the submarine, which

---

6   *The USS Hyman G. Rickover (SSN-709) was a Virginia-class nucle-ar-powered attack submarine and was the second submarine, after the first USS Hyman G. Rickover (SSN-709), that was not named after a United States city or town. [Wikipedia]*

I believe was about 30 feet below, I had to turn sideways to get through a tube and down steep stairs. I didn't go down more than three or four rungs on the ladder when I grabbed a man's foot that was coming down above me.

He said, "Hey, brother, what are you doing?"

I told him he needed to go back up, and then he asked why. Again, I asked him to go back up and not to ask any more questions. He finally allowed me to get out and once there, I saw the commander watching us. He asked me if something was wrong.

I said, "Yes, I'm claustrophobic, and there is no way I'm going down there. I cannot." I told him that I was fine, not to worry about me; I had a nice jacket to keep me warm.

He started talking me through it, in a way that I couldn't say no anymore. So, he went with me, and we got down to the bottom, which actually was just stacks of food boxes in the galley. I couldn't even stand straight up until I reached the end where I had to jump down, alongside the missiles. The galley was filled to the top with food boxes, and the crew literally eat the food down to the galley floor. This usually takes about 90 days and then they need to resurface to replenish their food supply. The tour lasted about an hour or so, but I was always looking for sunlight. I was very proud of myself at the end of that tour.

Later that afternoon, we left Norfolk aboard a U.S. Air Force aircraft for a four-and-a-half-hour flight to the home of the Air Warfare Center on Nellis AFB near Las Vegas, Nevada. Before boarding, I told our cadre that he was going to have a hard time beating our experience that day. He said, "Just wait." We had been told that on this flight, we were going to have the opportunity to observe an in-flight refueling operation for the first time. Well, actually, we got to do more than observe.

Our cadre asked me to come to the rear of the airplane with him. He told me to lie down on my stomach and look down a window with a nearby joystick. I looked into the window, right into the pilot's eyeballs in a plane below us. At a height of 30,000 feet, using a 60' pole that connected us, I started the descent of 3,000 gallons of highly flammable fuel into the plane below. Others on the flight were also able to give it a try. Afterwards, we disconnected, he waved and took off.

Back at Nellis AFB, we later saw that plane and another. We were told not to touch them. We could shoot guns, drive trucks or tanks, but we could not touch them because the skin of the aircraft was, and is, highly classified. Apparently, it is invisible to radar, and the Air Force did not want to take the chance that someone might guess the materials it was made out of.

Once we arrived at Nellis, we went directly to the Officer's Club to have dinner with many of the base's senior leaders. As spokesperson for the Air Force, I had the privilege of handing the commander a $2,000 check for his crew to have a party.

The next morning, Thursday, we ate breakfast in the Nellis dining hall with several enlisted members. Afterwards, we got to experience the same multimedia debriefing that they receive after combat training over the Nellis ranges. We learned that fighter and bomber pilots from all over the world train there. We toured the base's Threat Training Facility where we saw aircraft, missiles, tanks, and other military equipment that had been captured from enemy forces dating back to the Korean war.

Following lunch with some junior officers, we got to closely look at fighters and bombers that they had used during Desert Storm. We also had the opportunity to watch several fighter planes take off before being shown the hangar where they are stored. I'm not sure how many fighter planes they had, but there was a whole bunch of them. Our final stop was watching an aerial demonstration by their Air Force team, the Thunderbirds.

Area 51 was our next stop. Signs on the gate stated, "Shoot on sight." No questions asked. We were escorted inside.

While it didn't look like much on the ground, this is where they tested top secret aircraft. They drove us over the desert land to an area where bleachers were set up for us to sit and observe what was going on. All of a sudden, a small house in the distance exploded, followed by total silence. Seconds later, we heard a sonic BOOM! The planes were so much faster than the speed of sound and had that kind of precision.

Later that evening, we arrived in Fort Lewis to see the activities of the Army infantry. That afternoon, we left Nellis on a two-hour flight to Fort Lewis, Washington and that night they had a welcome reception for us before we headed to a local hotel.

On Friday morning, we were told that we were going to experience a soldier's day in the field, wearing our very own Army uniforms. Fort Lewis is the home of I Corps, America's Corps. We were shown all of the capabilities of I Corps soldiers and their equipment in action. We had the opportunity to actually fire state-of-the-art weapons (like we now see in Ukraine). One soldier called me over to his weapon that was already set up and told me to pull the trigger. I did so, and then he looked into his sight and congratulated me. I had achieved 80% destruction of a tank that I couldn't even see.

We also observed the artillery capabilities of the M109A3 Howitzer gun/weaponry and ate Meals Ready to Eat (MREs) along with the soldiers. They also showed us how they handled injuries in the field. Some of us were able to drive a M1 Abrams tank or the Army's High Mobility Multipurpose Wheeled Vehicle (HMMWV), and others took the chance to parachute jump; I did not.

We boarded an Air Force plane that afternoon on a two-hour flight to Camp Pendleton, California. Wherever we went, on a boat or a plane, Linda Tripp would always sit next to me. Her mother was Austrian, so she spoke German but had few opportunities to practice it until this trip. On the flight to Camp Pendleton, I asked her how she was doing this week and whether everything was going the way she had envisioned it.

Linda said, "No. Can you imagine the audacity of that PT guy?"

I asked her what had happened. She replied that when we signed up for this trip, we had to make a commitment to attend the entire week. No one was allowed to leave, that was in writing. He signed up like everyone else. Well, when we left for Fort Lewis, PT asked Linda to call his office and have a plane sent to Camp Pendleton to pick him up. I asked her how she had responded to him. She replied that she had been left speechless that he would ask such a thing. Well, PT left anyway and nothing could be done about it, but Linda was upset about the situation.

Upon arrival to Camp Pendleton, we were greeted by the U.S. Marine Corp at a reception that night. It was a long day as all the others had been, with at most, four hours of sleep a night. Sometimes we were so pumped up, that it took a while to fall asleep.

Saturday was our last day. After breakfast with some Marines, we received a brief presentation on the war-fighting Marine Expeditionary Forces (MEF) and its current operations. We got to interact with these young Marines of the MEF and were given the opportunity to drive their equipment and fire their weapon systems.

We then cruised along 17 miles of California coastline in an air-cushioned landing craft. We also rode over rough terrain in light armored vehicles and observed an exercise of Marine Corps combat service support (logistics) capabilities, commonly known as Force Recon. Lastly, we saw a demonstration of the Marine Air-Ground Task Force in action as they conducted urban operations in a state-of-the-art "Military Operations in Urban Terrain" facility.

That night was our farewell reception and dinner. The next morning, on Sunday, JCOC 59 ended with a mid-morning brunch where we were able to ask questions and provide any feedback about any of our experiences of the past week. Most participants left that day but I had spoken to General Schoomaker before I left and asked him if I could see the SEAL's training since we were so close by. He said sure, so after JCOC, I arranged to stay near Camp Pendleton and hosted a going away dinner of my own with Linda Tripp and the five cadres. We stayed an extra two days so we could observe the Navy SEAL training in San Diego. It was a once in a lifetime experience, and they were so appreciative. My guests sure let their hair down during those two days as the drinking and the language was R rated!

Right:
1) Aboard the USS Hyman Rickover submarine at JCOC.
2–3) My day with the Army at JCOC.

USS HYMAN G. RICKOVER
"COMMITTED TO EXCELLENCE"
709
SSN-709

My day at SEAL training on Coronado Island at JCOC.

Our Air Force cadre at Camp Pendleton.

CHAPTER 26

RETURNING HOME FROM JCOC

When I came back home, I wanted to fulfill the required obligations that I had agreed to. The civilians that had been picked were generally leaders in their communities and well connected. The academia that had previously been against the armed forces were now speechless and still obligated to go back to their respective universities and colleges to share what they had learned. My obligation was to make the community aware as to what the military does in more detail than is usually known. So I went to the *St. Petersburg Times* where I knew several members of management. I informed them of my commitment to share my experience at JCOC and wanted one of their reporters to write about it for me and that I would pay them. They sent one of their writers, and I shared the binder I was given, including the names and itinerary of my week at JCOC. She called the Pentagon to verify all that I had told her was accurate. It was a four-page article in the *St. Petersburg Times* in 1996.

Once I "graduated" from JCOC, I was given the option to join DOCA, the Defense Orientation Conference Association, an

Above photo: Stealth Fighter F117 being refueled.

offshoot of JCOC. Apparently many of the 60 participants were so impressed and had inquired if they could see what was done outside of the U.S., so that's why DOCA was created. It more or less had the same mission of JCOC but was international in nature.

About a year later, DOCA participants went to Honduras, El Salvador, and Nicaragua. We left Tampa, and I was flying first class in my usual seat (1B). Next to me was a guy that was acting so strange. He had a pen in his hand and was clicking it really fast, like a machine gun. He was not American, possibly Muslim, and this was during the period of time when hijackings were commonplace. I got up and went to the head flight attendant and suggested that she might want to inform the captain that the guy next to me was acting very strange. I was going by the motto, "If you see something, say something," so I told her about his constant clicking and perspiring.

I noticed some of the other flight attendants go back and forth and one of them must have said something to the pilot because I was told that he wanted to speak to me. So, I went to the front, like I was going to the bathroom and met the Captain. I told him that I didn't know what the issue was but something was going on, like he didn't want to be on the plane. The Captain thanked me for making him aware of the situation, and I went back to my seat, and nothing transpired.

Shortly before landing, the pilot came on the speaker and said, "I don't know how many of you have flown into Tegucigalpa but it is a very different experience. I want to make you aware that it is a very short landing and take-off strip. We have to fly through many S turns and very close to homes. You will be able to look into kitchens and see people eating in there. But don't worry, we are trained for this; we fly to this airport every day. Don't be concerned."

Now the guy next to me was really going nuts. So finally, I looked at him and said, "Tell me, what is the problem?"

He responded that he was from Lebanon and flew to Honduras often to do business and he so hated flying into that airport.

I told him, "Oh, God, I thought you were going to blow us up!"

He replied, "No, I'm just scared on the airplane!" He told me later that he flew into Tegucigalpa at least twice a year. After going through that landing, I understood his fear. It was a memorable flight.

DOCA lasted about a week where we visited and stayed in the American embassies or in hotels. Unlike me, I felt that most of the participants just wanted an excuse to be away and were not as interested in the mission of DOCA.

In Nicaragua, as we walked into our hotel, I saw bonfires on the roof and sharpshooters. When we approached the front desk to check in, the first thing I looked for was the emergency exit. I found it, and it was chained shut.

I said, "Guys, hold on. Before we check in here, we should make sure that the emergency exit is unlocked." The receptionist said no, it was locked for security.

I said, "Listen, do you want me to call the embassy or how do you want me to handle it? We are not going to sleep here if this is locked. We need an escape, after all, I mean there is a sharpshooter on the roof." So they unlocked it.

During our week, we met some Sandinistas or Contras, depending upon our location. We visited parts of the world, so different than the United States, that most never get to see.

Upon our return from DOCA, we had to send our report to the Pentagon. In the meantime, they had received a copy of the *St. Petersburg Times* newspaper article.

Soon after, the 12 participants of the DOCA trip were invited to the Pentagon. By then, the Secretary of Defense was Donald Rumsfeld, under President George W. Bush. We went into the Press Room, and we waited for then Defense Secretary Donald Rumsfeld to come in. When he did, unrehearsed, we all stood up and gave him a standing ovation. Secretary Rumsfeld had tears in his eyes.

He said, "I come here daily, and the media people try to tear me to shreds. I've never had a standing ovation." He was very appreciative and very touched. Rumsfeld was my hero.

The Defense Orientation Conference Association (DOCA) is a nationwide non-profit organization dedicated to continuing education in defense and national security affairs. Their members facilitate heightened awareness of how the nation's military forces contribute to the safety and security of the United States of America and its allies globally.

What we do: By focusing on issues and challenges in the areas of defense, foreign policy and national security, DOCA's membership of business and civic leaders provides a direct conduit of information to our local communities to enhance public understanding of the vital roles and capabilities of the men and women in the U.S. Armed Forces. Our members achieve this by engaging directly with representatives of the armed forces and government officials at military bases and embassies around the world by interacting with personnel both formally and informally at all levels, from new recruits up to the most senior commanders and government officials. Members then return home to share this information with their respective communities. Our members are passionate in supporting those who choose to serve. We continue to grow as the premier, non-partisan, defense support organization in the USA. [website]

My World Cruise

There comes the day when you long to go to far-away places. Once you are there, you find yourself lonely and desire to go back home.

ARRANGING MY TRIP AROUND THE WORLD

Sometime in early 2002, I was planning for Mary's and my upcoming 25th wedding anniversary in January 2003. I excitedly told Mary that I wanted to take her on a world cruise for four months.

Without hesitation, she responded, "Would you be upset if I didn't go?"

To which I replied, "No, as long as you won't be upset if I still go." Mary said she wouldn't be, and she meant it.

The next morning, I asked Mary what she did want for our wedding anniversary. Again, without hesitation she said, "New carpeting."

With surprise, I replied, "Be realistic. What do you really want?" That is exactly what Mary wanted. She knew that I would be gone for four months in early 2003 on the world cruise, so she hired an architect and started planning the renovations that included much more than new carpeting. She knew that I didn't like coming home to a mess and took advantage of my time away. God bless Mary.

Above photo: The M/S Seven Seas Mariner.

My original plan to take Mary on a world cruise had now changed to planning a solo trip. I tried to contact Cunard Line first because they had White Star Service, a high standard of customer service, but they never returned my call. After some research, I called the Radisson Cruise line number to arrange my trip and to discuss the fact that I was not willing to pay the marriage penalty tax for traveling alone. All cruises generally charge a hefty penalty for having only one person staying in a suite.

The saleswoman who answered the phone was very polite and happy to make my arrangements. When I explained that I would not pay the marriage penalty, she said that it was not possible to waive it.

My response was, "If you could have made that decision, you wouldn't have answered the phone. Please put me on with someone who can."

She transferred me to the Director of Sales who said the same thing. I reiterated that I would not be paying 50% more to travel solo, but that I would be happy to pay full price immediately, a year prior to the trip.

"I'm sorry sir, but I cannot do this for you," was his response.

"Well, I have another option," I continued. "I own several travel agencies and can take my 40 percent commission off the top, or you can make this happen. Which would you prefer?"

He sighed and said, "I can't make this decision right now. Can you give me a little time?"

"I can wait for you to let me know but I want to finalize the trip. How long are you talking?" I asked.

"It may take a month or two," he answered.

"Alright, let me know," I said and hung up.

He called three days later to say, "You got it!"

And that is how I secured passage on the Radisson Seven Seas World Cruise on their Mariner ship in 2003. In addition to this world cruise, I wanted to make some other stops, so I also purchased a first-class plane ticket to travel around the world. It was offered for a surprisingly reasonable price as long as I traveled in the same direction and made no more than three stops. This was my way to add other excursions that were not offered on the Seven Seas cruise.

CHAPTER 28

FINALLY THE DAY COMES

In February 2003, I finally set off on my world trip. I start off with my first journal entry but throughout this section, you will find my emails to my wife and daughters in italics. I sent them regularly during this trip and have included the more pertinent emails as additional information.

JOURNAL ENTRY

The day finally has come, and I am sitting in the Crown room at the Tampa airport. My Honey, (that is what I call my lovely wife of 25 years and 37 days), and one of my wonderful daughters, Courtney, just dropped me off. A few crocodile tears, lots of hugs and kisses, and thank God my bags are checked to Sydney, Australia. It is my hope to find them there in 46 hours, which is how long it will take to get there. My first leg is Dallas and from there on Korean Air to Seoul for a 17-hour layover, and then on to Sydney. The flying conditions could not be better. The Department of Homeland Security declared code orange, and therefore, security at all the airports worldwide is extra tight. A comfort!

Above photo: An open–air market in Seoul, Korea.

It has been a dream since I was at the Benedictine Abbey in Melk at the age of 12 to see the world. The day has arrived, and can you believe it, someone who grew up in Austria without electricity, telephone, television, running hot or cold water, and with sparse rations of food, is communicating via the information superhighway? I must be careful not to end up as road kill, on this fast-moving global network.

There were a lot of goodbyes and best wishes from family, friends, team members, and guests. Many people I spoke with have been to some of the places I am planning to visit. I have been given more advice as to what to do and what not to do, that it is almost like being back in Melk. 18 countries and 27 cities in total not including Europe. Most of my time will be on a ship in Asia, India, and Africa. The companion, around the world ticket, leaves me flexibility to venture out on side trips in order to collect unscheduled memories.

By now, you might have discovered that I am a better story teller than writer, but this will not discourage me to continue at my next stop. So long for now.

The last message on CNN, as I was leaving the Crown Room to make my way to the gate, was "North Korea does have a nuclear bomb, and the delivery system to reach the US." Well as we say in Dunedin: Bon Voyage... Dude!

The flight to Dallas was uneventful, however, at check-in for Korean Air, my Asian experience began. The appearance, postures, uniforms, accents, and the smiling eye contact from everyone I came in contact with was exceptionally friendly and helpful; a sheer delight. Being a member of the global service business myself, I always like to see how others handle special requests, in this case, my own.

Due to the fact that I had a 17-hour layover in Seoul, I wished for information about city sightseeing as well a room reservation at the new airport hotel. I made my wishes known as I was escorted to my seat number 1C in first class. No sooner than I had finished spraying mineral water mist on my face, there was the Purser with a gift book with everything about Korea and then some. Phone numbers, addresses, and photos of Korean steam baths (a must for weary travelers). Also, this lovely young lady, whose name I was not able to read on her name tag, much less pronounce, had already called her supervisor in Seoul and the hotel to make my reservation. Amex guarantee not required.

On the plane, a Korean lady of about 50 to 80 years old, was sitting next to me. Age is hard to tell for the most part, especially for me. Her German and English was about as fluent as my Korean. My only way to communicate was through eye contact and a slight but dignified bowing of my head forward. This was very helpful, and as a result, I really had a memorable dinner. I had all four flight attendants and my neighbor assist me with the hot pepper paste and the sesame oil to "smear and mush onto my bowl of rice." This was to be eaten with green and yellow roots that had the consistency of kohlrabi (turnip). Perhaps the staff was so helpful since the plane was virtually empty. First and business class had a few passengers, but coach was deserted. One wonders if CNN had anything to do with this, or is it the wardrobe and the nice haircut of the charming North Korean Dictator who stands about as tall as Lindsey? Lindsey was my dog!

I was told that another flight mate on this 777/200 was Jackie Chan. His schedule was of out of sync with the rest of us. He slept when we were eating, and he ate when we were sleeping. Boy, did he use that hot pepper paste onto his meal. It comes in a tube, sort of like toothpaste. All you have to do is squeeze and yell, FIRE!

Well, I thought the time had come for one more squirt of mineral spray to freshen up and try to arrive in Korea the best I could with what I had to work with. I had four big suitcases that I had picked up from my home and sent to Los Angeles to be delivered to my state room on the Seven Seas Mariner. They would be waiting for me when I started my cruise in Sydney, Australia. All I had was a backpack that I had borrowed from Casey. There was no room for a change of clothes so I wondered if they sold disposable garments at the airport. As it was, I purchased a few items in Korea, and more in Sydney, until I boarded the ship.

I did the same thing in reverse, but when I got back, eight suitcases were returned to my home. I purchased lots of souvenirs and gifts for the girls, Mary, and myself.

EMAIL

Re: Happy Valentine's Day Honey Bunny!

Hi my girls,

Korea is wonderful. The nicest, most polite, and courteous people I have ever met. It is 13:18 hours on Valentine's Day and I just returned from downtown Seoul where I have been sightseeing and exploring since we arrived at 5:10 a.m. this morning. I slept on the plane, and the ride over was great. Absolutely no jet lag.

My nose is in overdrive, and I am trying all kinds of Asian herbs. Presently, I am in the 1st class lounge of Korean Air. Casey would love it. Hundreds of free computers, showers, massages, slumber rooms, etc. My massage is in one hour from now.

I have started quite a journal, but must yet figure out how to send it. I hooked up with a lawyer from Greenville, SC on his way to Bangkok. Also with a 10-hour layover. We keep watching each other's luggage.

As I said, I am so glad I came here, I really love the people. The markets, all outdoors, are all we ever heard of, and if it were not for the Siberian blast that covers this peninsula, it would be a balmy day. Temperature 15 degrees, but sunny.

My dinner last night was a bowl of rice to be blended with seaweed, dried anchovies, sesame oil and hot pepper paste. I wrote more about my Asian meals in my journal, but so far, I have lost four pounds.

CHAPTER 29

SYDNEY, AUSTRALIA

From Korea, I flew to Sydney to stay just shy of two weeks to visit with the son of a good friend of mine and to see the sites while there. So, this worked out well as I was to start my cruise in Sydney on February 21, 2003, and head off to see the many ports of call around the world through April 18, 2003.

EMAIL

The flight from Seoul to Sydney was rather uneventful and I had the same dining choices as yesterday and the day before. I wonder if they ever run out of dried anchovies. One cannot imagine how glad I was when I saw my luggage on the carousel. My cab driver, fresh from Ghana, could not find the Best Western Hotel Capitol Square. It took $60 to drive around and around the same city blocks before I spotted it. The hotel was simply awful, and in spite of the fact that I had not slept in over 70 hours, I refused to stay there. Sydney is booked out this weekend due the annual Gay and Lesbian festival and the planned anti-war protest for the next day.

Above photo: Sydney's Opera House.

I had to use all my tricks in my book to find an apartment at the Radisson Hotel. It is actually quite nice and the General Manager went way overboard when he found out that I was scheduled on the world cruise. As I always said, if there is a will, there is a way. "No" was not an option today. I think from reading these lines, I am somewhat testy, must be I am overly tired. I took half of an Ambien and slept till 8 a.m. local time, about 12 hours.

Sunday

Well, they all came. From all over Australia and elsewhere, there were protesters en masse. I felt really vulnerable due to the way I dressed. In a t-shirt and blue jeans, I was the best dressed man in Sydney today. A Sydney Pass for three days, $90, was a great investment. I already got my money's worth. Took the ferry to Parramatta, about a 2-hour round trip. Very scenic! The rest of the day, I rode the city transport, hop-on-hop-off. Went to the Chinese market place and got a watch for $15, pants for $10, another t-shirt for $6. My honey would love this place. In all, a very busy and eventful day. Dinner at Darling Harbor. Kangaroo does not taste like chicken. Got a small flask of bourbon and retreated to my flat.

One last thing about Seoul, a city of 3.8 million people, is spotless. I never even saw one cigarette butt or paper anywhere. They had more cleaners and workers everywhere. It was truly impressive. Sydney on the other hand is a different story. Well, tomorrow it is out to Bondi Beach. Good night for now.

Monday

Finally, I am well rested. I got up at 6 a.m. and organized all those silly little details that make life on the road more enjoyable. Went to the market to get coffee, milk, breakfast feed, as they call it here so that I don't have to go to the "slimming" salon, and then boarded the Bondi Explorer. Bondi Beach is Australia's most famous beach. I just went for the sights and not to swim.

In fact, I took the round trip twice. The first time for orientation, and the second time for the suggested Bondi to Bronte Beach walk, normally 45 minutes along the most beautiful shoreline up and down cliffs. It did rain, however, and I had to backtrack and found shelter with six Austrians. They are everywhere, one just cannot get away from them.

I started out from Circular Quay, which is also the terminal from which my ship is leaving on Friday the 21st. Then onto WOOL-LOOMOOLOO BAY, this is not misspelled.

By now, my favored place. They call it Loo for short. I got off the bus and had a memorable bite at Harry's Café de Wheels. It is the most famous food stand in Sydney. Here since 1939, it is right next to the Australian Naval docks.

Their specialty is "Tiger," a pie with green pea mash. It is a small meat pie topped with squished mashed potatoes, then they pile green pea mash on top of it and make a hole in the middle, which they fill with gravy. Not exactly my most favored dish, but at least it was not hamburgers. I took some photos of the place including the menu. From there, I took the next hop-on to Kings Cross, Rushcutter's Bay, Double Bay onto the beaches of Bondi, Tamarama, Bronte, and Coogee. After that, back to Sydney.

I now have the right adapter from the hotel to get on the net. That is why I am writing while the sending is good. This evening, I am taking a ferry to cruise Sydney Harbor after dark. By the way, Casey, your backpack is a lifesaver. It will have many stories to tell when we get home. It told me it will tell it to all "those people." You would not believe how many backpackers there are here. There are more backpacking places than fast food stores combined. Everyone's stocking up to go to the outback or the bush, literally. You will see on the postcards, which I sent, about Sydney's Harbor bridge or the "Coat Hanger" as they call it. People can walk up to the top and back for $150 per person, and many do. I think I will not anytime soon.

Honey, if you think it is appropriate, you may share some or all of these notes with people at work. Also, you are welcome to censor some if you feel it necessary. I am mostly writing for you and the girls.

Wednesday

It is 8 p.m. and I am sitting at Quayside at Zenbu, a waterfront restaurant at Darling Harbor. I just had a Chinese massage in public, open air and all, but so what, everyone else did too. Fully clothed in Aussie cargo shorts and my Brooks Brothers shirt. It was simply fantastic. The guy was great, and even during the $50 massage, he upsold me on the Zen cleansing for an extra $19, well worth it. Sydney is by now, without a doubt, my favorite place.

First thing this morning I found the wash house and dropped off three shirts for wash, press and fold. They do not use starch in the wash, only if you send it to the dry cleaners will you get starch. So...no starch. I had my shirts dry cleaned once, what a horrible experience. Furthermore, since I have been on the road for so long without accommodations, I only I had two pair of dirty undies. Certainly not enough for a bag wash for $12, therefore I tossed them, and bought three new ones at the Chinese market for $3. I guess I could get used to disposable undies, right, Honey?

At noon, I met John McGhee, Jr. at Circular Quay, right where he works in the tallest and most beautiful building in that harbor, and the same place where I have been spending a lot of time the last three days. We went to Aqua Luna, also in the harbor, waterfront, of course. Is there anything else in Sydney? Aqua Luna is where the elite meet in Sydney for their noonday meal. John, dressed like his father, and exactly how an investment banker should look, made me feel like a country hick. Nevertheless, we had a marvelous few hours, a great lunch, and I told him many of the stories and events which I had shared with his dad. He is a lovely person, and I hope to see him again one day. John and his girlfriend are planning to have children after they visit Europe next Easter.

It is the middle of summer here, even though Mardi Gras is next week and therefore, Easter seems removed. Just thinking of Casey who is in the middle of a blizzard, and I am in the middle of summer, without humidity. I just finished my Thai beef salad and am still hungry...wonder what my nice server will bring next.

A young lady just stopped by my table and wanted to give me a massage. Yes, while I was eating. This is the first time in my life that I declined such a thing. Essentially for two reasons. First, and most importantly, because I just had a most terrific massage, and secondly, because I was eating. I did, however, invite her back for dessert. They just go from table to table and rub people's neck and back during dinner. I love these Asian customs. Imagine doing this at the Bon Appétit!

After lunch, I signed up for a historic walking tour of the rock, the oldest part of Sydney.

Since the town is a mere 215 years old, the tour lasted only 90 minutes. When I told the people that my Vienna was 900 years old, they thought I was lying. Can you blame them?

By now, I have learned to get around town on the water by ferries, and this is how I went to Watson's Bay. The oldest fishing village in Australia, 1788, where not much has changed. Three cafés and gelato shops. Two markets, one sells food and fruit, and the other sells fruit and food. What a place of opportunity for an entrepreneur. Thousands and thousands of people come through there every day to look over the cliffs into the Pacific Ocean and the entrance to Sydney's Harbor. I took some photos there.

You would not believe it, I had finished my second course, a very lusty, but not too spicy Asian roll with shredded beef, as Coco, the masseuse, came back and started giving me an after-dinner rub. I will never forget this day. A fabulous Chinese massage before dinner and another one right after. I don't think I will ever enjoy a meal without major Asian rubs. What a life! I don't know why, but after Coco finished with me, the rest of the customers applauded. By now, I am so accustomed to it, that I found it quite normal, especially since many other people had rubs here, either before, during, or after their meals.

Also, last night I ate right next door at Jordon's. A little more up market, dinner for one, $120 Australian dollars (the exchange was 60 cents U.S. to one Australian dollar), but also very memorable. I had the seafood tower. Everything that swims or crawls under or near the water was served. The green and blue swimmer crabs were especially delightful. This restaurant is so popular that on weekends and on holidays, they add a $3 surcharge per guest, just for the privilege of dining there. My waiter, Trevor, a real "Sydney-sider" (native of Sydney) from the alternative lifestyle side, invited me as his special guest of honor on their float during next week's Gay and Lesbian Mardi Gras parade. I had to respectfully decline since my ship was leaving the day after tomorrow.

At any rate, Jordon's is on the list for the return visits. In addition, the hostess, whose parents are from Graz, Austria and who speaks fluent German, also added to the evening's experience.

People are simply nice here, totally uncomplicated and real down to earth. One of the things that makes Sydney so special is that Australia is so far away from everywhere else in the world, that not too many people come here. It is not overrun with tourists, and those that venture on that long journey, find their true reward at the end of it. If I have not mentioned it, Sydney is comprised of people from over 140 countries. Talk about cosmopolitan, inter-continental, and global!

To think that it has just been a week since I left my loved ones and Tampa. It seems like a lifetime of experiences and impressions. So glad I came. Good night, journal.

Thursday

Well, this is the last night in Sydney and the time to board the ship, my home for the next couple of months has arrived. I finished some mundane details today such as restocking medication, getting laundry from the wash house, etc.

I visited the National Maritime Museum, which is wonderful to see, and I learned much about the expeditions to Antarctica. Talk about a challenge! Also, I found it interesting that I am not the first person to discover Australia on my own. Captain Cook, when he first arrived here in 1770 to discover Australia, also came without Mrs. Cook. From what I understand, she stayed home and remodeled their hut.

That's it for tonight.

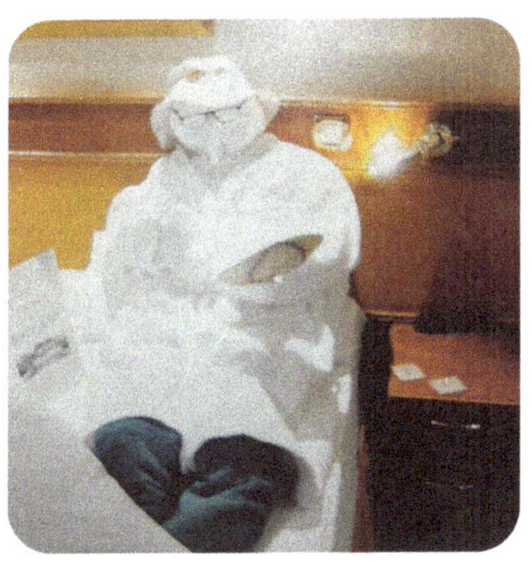

CHAPTER 30

ABOARD THE M/S SEVEN SEAS MARINER

EMAIL

Friday

We left Sydney at 19:00 on the dot. As required by maritime law, we had a life drill at 18:15 and it was very thorough and well done. Good thing, too, because now two hours and 15 minutes later, we are in a gale warning, and the wind speed is 89.2 km/h.

Now I wish to tell you about the ship. It is a triple WOW< WOW< and WOW again.

I boarded at 14:00 and registered through all the stations, security, ship registration, and check-in. My stateroom is 1029, a very lucky number indeed. It is on the top floor of accommodations, and as with all suites, has an outside balcony starboard side. This is the preferred side from Japan back to South Africa. I will be able to see

Above photo: My favorite towel character in my
Stateroom 1029.

all the countries passing by rather than just looking out to sea. By the way, on this next leg, it will be the second time that I will be crossing the equator. All in all, it will be five times during this trip. There is a ritual for doing this. I must read up on it.

The interior is nothing short of world class. It reminds me of the luxury of the Grand Hotel in Vienna. Highly polished wood, crystal, a marble bath, and the finest linen. The halogen lights were on, the music was low on sentimental classical, fresh flowers everywhere, the champagne on ice, and the freshest fruit in a crystal bowl on the table. A welcome letter inviting me to all kinds of receptions and welcome parties that night.

It was still raining very much on the outside, but the interior was so warm and welcoming that the weather just added to the atmosphere. The only people missing are my Honey, Courtney and Casey. Well, next time, you don't think we are not doing this again?

Alicia, a young stewardess from Poland, has been assigned to take care of my on-board needs. She is very pretty and very friendly as is everyone else so far.

Also, I met Ilse from Stuttgart, and her husband from Berlin. They are the dance instructors on-board. They travel the world giving dance lessons and double as dance partners. Their home is on Pine Key in the Florida Keys. They wasted no time to introduce me to everyone at the reception, and I was surprised as to how many people are from Florida that boarded the ship. Paulette, on-board to give cooking classes, is also an author who has published over a dozen cookbooks. Exhausted, after having met so many people all at once, I went to the Signature restaurant by myself for dinner. The Sevruga caviar with puree of celery was excellent with a small glass of Puilly Fume. Rack of lamb, with an assortment of sauteed mushrooms and a potato slice, was outstanding as well with a few sips of Cotes du Rhone. Fortunately, the portions are rather small, even though one may request as many supplements as desired, and I, of course, skipped dessert. I was still hungry when I left, and this is a good thing. I do not wish to gain weight, and right now the gale force winds are just howling around the observation deck where I am sitting all alone with the nautical instrument readouts. I give locations so you all can look it up on the interactive website of the ship. Honey, please tell Courtney and Casey how to do this.

When I boarded the ship on the first day, Ilse and her husband greeted me and showed me the way to my state room. Afterwards, I went into the dining room where the maître d' said, "Do you want to dine by yourself, or do you prefer to join some people?"

And I said, "Well, it's my first night here, so yes, I'd like to maybe sit with some people."

So, he put me at a table of 10 with nine women where I was peppered with questions. "What's your name?" "Where are you from?" "How many times have you been around the world?" One lady said she had been on these cruises 25 times. And I replied, "Why, don't you remember from one year to the next?"

I learned that some passengers take a leave of absence from their nursing home and get a credit. Apparently, it's cheaper to be on the ship with all the amenities in the world. They come for just a change of scenery. Most of them never left the ship while in port because they had gone so many times before.

After dinner, I went down to the bar where there was music. I was one of the first people to get there. So, I was sitting at the bar, having an after-dinner drink and this older woman came up to me and said, "I would like to dance."

I looked at her and said, "So dance."

She then said, "No, I want to dance with you. Aren't you the dance host?"

I replied, "No, I'm a passenger just like you. I had to pay to sit here."

I met Bill Bates, who had been a cruise director for many years, and he knew all the other directors and staff from many other ships. At that time, he lived in Carmel, California but was a goodwill ambassador for the cruise line, traveling with free accommodations. He would help the guests feel at home and would answer questions about all manner of things, ports of call, excursions, and more. He also worked for the Carmel newspaper, doing the caricatures in the newspaper's Arts section.

He traveled on a world cruise once a year, drawing all along the way. On our cruise, he would sit in the passageway every morning and sketch the passengers as they came by. I would often sit with him, and he would tell me all sorts of stories about many of them. At the end of each cruise, he would bind all of his sketches into a book that he would offer for sale. It was a great memento of the trip, and I, of course, bought one too.

Bill's wife was Chinese, and they also had a home in Cape Town, South Africa. So, I met her when we arrived in Cape Town toward the end of my cruise. Bill was also a solo traveler as was Father Bob, a Catholic priest from Michigan. The three of us became friends and travel companions on this trip.

EMAIL

Rowing, rowing and still rowing...

We are for the next three days and nights in the Coral Sea on our way to Papua, New Guinea.

I am meeting new people every day and am collecting interesting vignettes for my journal. The website from davidonna.com will keep you better informed, at least pictorially.

I had a visit with Peter Einfeld, a consultant for Radisson. He has done 35 world cruises on other ships and is on board to pamper the around-the-world passengers. He gave me interesting statistics:

There are fewer than six ships doing world cruises in the luxury category. The combined total of all passengers worldwide, that do the whole trip is fewer than 1,000. A quite select market. His role is to bring them from other ships to the Radisson. I was wondering as to why all world travelers know each other so well. Now I understand. I hope to get to know them as well.

Unfortunately, we lost a guest last night at dinner in the dining room. I wish Bill could have seen this. They sat the guest in a wheelchair, propped him up, and rolled him into the freezer. Another lady left us in New Zealand, we think it was by suicide. She just stopped taking her medications. One never knows what people are thinking, and why they are doing the things they are doing. And in Noumea, a lady was left behind in the island's hospital. What a frightful thought! Having met the French ship's doctor, I can understand her decision, however. More about that later.

Well, I must go back to rowing, the break is over.

CHAPTER 31

PAPUA, NEW GUINEA

EMAIL

Friday

We arrived at 7 a.m. to a most beautiful island after a long sea voyage. Boy, was I glad to see land, palm trees blowing gently in the breeze and many natives that have come out to see the ship pull into the overseas dock in Madang, Papua New Guinea.

The last few days and nights, I noticed my attitude deteriorating by the nautical mile. I felt confined onto a tiny island in the middle of the Solomon Sea with 421 inhabitants. Progressively, I spent more and more time in my state room and wanted to see fewer and fewer people. My feelings were nothing unusual from what I am being told, that many people were feeling the same way.

At any rate, I was glad to set my feet on terra firma and explore this little paradise. It helped that I had attended a symposium about the history, culture, religion, and geography about New Guinea.

Above photo: My first Papuan lunch invitation.

215

This was the reason why I did not wear my Bon Appétit polo shirt. These people are direct descendants of mostly former, and yes, some still current, cannibals. Contrary to Noumea, the locals and natives are exceptionally friendly, helpful and polite. Being the cynic that I am, I was wondering if that was due to the fact that they saw in me their next meal walking down the street. Dr. Dieter Galler lectured about the long-term effects of consuming a diet of humans. By the way they don't boil them, they bake them, perhaps healthier. It will ultimately begin to affect the protein in their brain, so much so, that over time, the brain cells begin to deteriorate and pulverize, caused by the now well identified side effect of the rare Kuru disease, UMU, a hostile stare without emotions and very little movement of the facial muscles.

Well, you can imagine, with this bit of diagnostic medical knowledge, I proceeded most cautiously through town with all my senses on high alert. There is a great deal of unimaginable poverty and, in spite of that, it is a peaceful place unless there is political unrest, and there was none today. Bill Bates, my artist friend, and I went to the market place, and he attracted quite a crowd as he sketched a local woman selling peanuts. By now, I had been off the ship for about one hour, had seen all the sights and taken the shuttle to the Madang resort hotel. The temperature had climbed to a level that reminded me of an oven, and I felt it would be wise to return to the ship. The first thing I noticed when I went onto land this morning was that all the locals had, what appeared to be, bleeding gums. In fact, I took a photo of the immigration officer right next to the Welcome sign in port.

This picture tells the story. Bleeding gums are the result of chewing betel nuts. But the warning sign, advising that Malaria is currently rampant on the island, was further reason for my very short visit.

When we arrived in a port, I generally tried to be one of the first to get off the ship to get away from the crowds. Upon arrival in Papua, the first sign I saw said: "Malaria is endemic in Papua New Guinea. Appropriate preventive medications are recommended should you leave the ship."

There was a guy that stood by the ship who welcomed me and had, what looked like, bleeding gums. He said to me, "Can I take you to lunch?" They had told us on the ship that, to this day, cannibalism is common there. So I thanked him for the offer but went on my way. I learned that the natives chew on betel nuts to get high, and when they do this often, their saliva slowly turns red, which is why I thought it was blood at first.

I then walked to their market where everyone, and their wares, were on the ground. One of the interesting items sold there were penis covers made by the natives. All the women onboard the ship bought them.

It is my understanding that the local tribal chief, who is Oxford educated, was the guest of honor of the Captain of another ship that stopped here. When presented with the menu in the dining room, he very quickly looked it over and closed it. When asked about his choice for the meal, he replied that he would rather order from the passenger list. Most everyone present thought he was kidding.

I heard another story about a Papua son who asked his father, "If there was a helicopter crash, how would you eat the human remains?"

His father replied, "Just like shellfish, you eat them from the inside out."

Then there is, of course, the Chimbu Skeletal Tribe's (another local tribe) handshake. It is a sign of peace, one that cannot be declined. The Chimbu warrior will put his hands between your legs and very gently squeeze your testicles. When he had the first female encounter he said, "So sorry, Sir, about your loss." We are told that homosexuality is widespread in Melanesia, Micronesia, Polynesia, and all the other lesser-known islands in this part of the world.

CHAPTER 32

ROUGH SEAS

EMAIL

Saturday

I have been in the computer lounge for over an hour. I am still the only person in this large room with classical music competing with the gale-force winds outside. The ship sails under the French flag, and therefore, the captain is French as well. He just came on the intercom and advised us that the ship will be pitching. I am beginning to feel this action. I tried to go outside but there was no way I could stand up without my clothes being torn off my body. It is getting worse. There are no icebergs, I hope!

I think it was Homer who said, "It is the journey that is more important than the destination." Well, with this thought in mind, I will retire to 1029, my home for the next two months.

Above photo: Updates on ship's TV channel.

Sunday

By now it is Sunday morning at about 3:15 am, and I must have fallen asleep, or so it seemed. I was awakened by the fact that I slid towards my highly polished headboard, and touched it with my head against it, in an abrupt fashion. I had left the drapes open, and I saw water splashing up to the 10th floor of the ship. I turned on the ship's channel on the TV and saw that the prevailing winds, head on, were now in excess of 100 km/h, with gusts going much higher than that. What great fun. I could not help thinking of Courtney on the Windsurf in Positano. All in all, I slept perhaps 2-3 hours combined, and when I got up, it was total fog. I did go to breakfast and had just a few slices of fruit, and a spoonful of corned beef hash. It does feel better.

Incidentally, I have transferred 36 photos from my camera, and deleted the smart card. The photos actually stayed. I am trying to send this message via a zip drive onto the ship's computer and from there onto AOL. And hopefully to you.

This afternoon I will attend a course in celestial navigation with heavy fog; I think that will be interesting. There are two more courses in chart plotting and direction finding.

As I find my way around this ship, I find more and more Austrian staff members. It is amazing how they do get around. The Hotel Director is also from Austria. Pretty soon we will have German lessons on board.

Last night, Rabbi Marti Kornreich held a Sabbath service, where all were welcome. Today is mass at 5 p.m. This evening is formal night. There is a reception at 6 p.m.

You may remember the woman who asked me to dance the first night of the cruise. I hadn't see her for a while. As we visited countries, I purchased and dressed in customary outfits of the country. I was quite noticeable in Japanese kimonos or whatever. Sometime during the trip, she came up and asked me to have dinner with her. I said, sorry, and told her I was booked for the next two weeks. I continued to come to dinner in a variety of native attire for weddings, funerals or other special occasions in beautiful silk and velvet fabrics. It was so much more comfortable than a monkey suit or tuxedo.

My usual routine was to go down before dinner, stand at the bar, and maybe sip on an umbrella drink. Other passengers often asked me to join their tables. I would consistently reply, "Sorry, but I'm already oversubscribed."

It had been several weeks, maybe a month now since I had met the persistent woman, and she came to me and said, "Peter, I have to have dinner with you."

I replied, "Okay, why is that?"

"Because I will be dying of cancer before I get back to Colorado," she responded.

I couldn't refuse at that point. The ship had all kinds of dining rooms where we could go anytime, 24 hours a day. But there was one gourmet dining room where we needed to make a reservation because it had limited seating, maybe 80 to 100 seats. She said she would make us a reservation there but I insisted on doing it. I went to the maître d' and requested a reservation for two, two days later. He asked if I wanted a nice table for two, and I replied, "No, two at a table for 12."

Two days later, she and I were the first ones to arrive at that table. We didn't know who the other 10 people to be seated were. The server came over and asked me, "What would you like to drink?"

I said, "I'll take a Campari with soda."

And she said, "What is that?"

I told her it was an aperitif, so she ordered the same drink. Then, two ladies from Las Vegas that I had seen from time to time on the ship joined our table. They typically wore t-shirts with pictures of breasts and bikinis on them, and that night was no different. Of course, they sat next to me and started a typical conversation.

One said, "Howdy, how are you doing? Where are you from?"

So, I told them I was from Vienna, Austria and asked if they had ever been there.

One looked at the other and said, "Have we ever been there?"

The other replied, "Is Austria on the ocean?"

I replied, "No, it's on the Danube, not the ocean."

The one who asked replied, "Oh, well I guess we haven't been there if it's not on the ocean."

Meanwhile, my "date" got jealous and hit me in the arm, and said, "You're with me, don't talk to them!"

Shortly thereafter, John Scully, the former president of PepsiCo and the former CEO of Apple Inc. came to our table. He was the guy who replaced Steve Jobs. Now retired, he lectured on cruises and around the world. And another couple came, and we were all introducing ourselves around. My "date" did it again, hitting me and reminding me that I was with her. The drinks came, I took a sip, put the glass down, and then said, "Oh my God, I forgot my medication. I have to go back to my suite."

I left and never went back. Instead, I ordered room service and had caviar, smoked salmon, liver, a beer, and a salad. It was a marvelous dinner, all by myself.

EMAIL

Hi my Honey and Girlies...

The person who presented a symposium about the political and economic situation in Asia and the Pacific today is Dr. Dieter

Galler. He romanced his then girlfriend, and now wife, Mercedes, who lived in Dunedin, Florida, and who has eaten many times at her very favorite restaurant, Bon Appétit. As you can see, I am always working and establishing new contacts. Of course, during his next lecture on board, he will tell all the ship's passengers about Dunedin and how wonderful Bon Appétit is.

I love you very much while cruising the Coral Sea.

P.S.: Courtney, when we are sailing in Guam, we will be in the deepest waters of any ocean. It is 1,000 feet deeper than Mount Everest is high. Just thinking about vertigo.

EMAIL

Today, we are sailing towards Kobe, Japan, which is another 24 hours away.

It is raining, which provided the proper setting for lectures in the morning by Dr. Dieter and Dr. Barbara. Her husband's lecture series is finished and all three will be departing in Kobe for new talent to arrive. Other passengers, Heinrich, Mary Van Schreiner, and I had an interesting lunch where we shared many religious stories from our collective monastic experiences. Heinrich also spent seven years in a Benedictine monastery in Austria.

Sometime during the next 24 hours, we will be going from summer to winter. The temperature in Kobe is about freezing. I am being told that there are many stories about myself circulating around the ship. My standard phrase, when asked is, I am a solo traveler but certainly not a single traveler, and contrary to some of the other passengers, I am not looking for a nurse with a purse. I was told, the reason why so many people wish to get to know me is not because of my great looks and interesting background, but merely because I can complete a sentence, I still have my hearing, and I drive at night. This might give you an indication about some of my shipmates.

Like the hippie doctor from Asheville, who dresses like a Vietcong and runs around in these loose pajamas on formal nights, she is wondering why even the gentleman dance hosts won't ask her to dance. You can get the flavor, sea days get to us, and people start to talk.

The day after tomorrow, I will be taking the bullet train to Kyoto to spend a night in a typical Japanese guest house, a Ryokan, which has been in the same family for five generations. We are being forewarned, no beds, just mats and futons. I am trying to sell my prepaid ticket, but no takers so far. Just kidding, I think. Whose idea was this anyway?

CHAPTER 33
KOBE, JAPAN

In Kobe, Japan, a small group of us had the opportunity to stay for one night in a Ryokan, loosely translated as a guest house, that dates back centuries. We were each assigned our own Geisha. Mine took me to a room where there was nothing, not a chair, not a bed, nothing, except in the corner there was a wooden cover on the floor. I didn't know what it was, a urinal or a spittoon? It was their version of a hot tub, which I was instructed to get into. I could barely clear my shoulders, and the water went up to my neck. While in there, she brought me a towel so I could get dry and dress. At dinner, we sat low to the ground, which wasn't exactly comfortable. Back in my room that evening, my Geisha brought in a blow-up mattress and all the bedding. She then had me lie on it and gave me a wonderful massage.

While there, I had to change my slippers, probably half a dozen times. When I first walked in, when I crossed a bridge, and whenever I entered my room. It was a unique experience, and I'm glad I did it, but I wouldn't do it again.

Above photo: The geishas and I...

EMAIL

I am, as usual, expected at church services, Father Bob told me at lunch. I asked him what the sermon is going to be about: Isaiah, the story about the lion sleeping with the lamb. I asked him to be excused since I know the story. I expected the lamb to have a sleepless night. This may be a good time to go to exercise class and try to skip afternoon tea and cookies, which is the meal of the day.

Just one more thing, now whenever I think of food, I cannot help but think back to the cannibals in New Guinea.

My guestroom in the ryokan in Kobe, Japan

CHAPTER 34
EXTRA DAYS IN SAIGON

While I was on the trip, there was an outbreak of SARS. The SARS virus was blamed on Vietnam, but it actually broke out in China. When we got to Ha Long Bay, Vietnam, I had prearranged to be picked up by a Russian helicopter to go to Hanoi with a couple of other people from the ship. The Captain never made daily announcements before 10:00 am.

When we arrived in Ha Long Bay, I heard the anchor being lowered. I mean, this makes a lot of noise because it's a huge anchor for that ship. However at 8:00 am that morning, the Captain came on the speaker and said that due to an outbreak of SARS in Vietnam, we were not going to stay for the helicopter trip to Hanoi. They were going to lift the anchor again and travel further down into Hong Gai, Da Nong and make some extra stops. As a result, we stayed an extra couple of days in Saigon, which by then was Ho Chi Minh City. So, it was okay. We lived so far away from the real world on that ship. There was never a day, or an hour, when I was concerned about SARS.

Above photo: My taxi in Ho Chi Minh City.

You know, the interesting thing was that no one on the ship had mentioned anything about SARS. My friend in Singapore had told me about it, just around Easter time. He said his kids had not had school for the last week of their semester because there was some sort of virus going around. From there, we were headed to Vietnam. My daughter, Courtney, sent me an email that SARS was breaking out. Nobody on the ship had any idea. I reprinted Courtney's e-mail from the World Health Organization and gave a copy to the ship's Captain. The company in the States never told the Captain about it.

"Listen, do you know anything about the SARS?" I asked.

The Captain replied, "No, it's up in China but now they blame it on Vietnam. That's why we left early from Halong Bay."

I responded that he should read what my daughter had read in the newspaper in the States.

He contacted Radisson's headquarters, who contacted the Center for Disease Control in Atlanta. They advised the company that the SARS virus originated in Hanoi, and we should not go there under any circumstances.

The ship had a capacity of 700 passengers when fully booked plus the crew. By this time, we were down to less than 300 passengers with 400 crew members. It was wonderful. There were two reasons for this. One, the war in Iraq and two, the SARS virus.

EMAIL

I had the opportunity to hear the President's speech to the nation, and I am glad that we are finally beginning to see the end. As an aside, while we were in Beijing, that rainy Sunday morning when Tiananmen Square was closed to traffic, the new Premier of China was elected while we were standing in the rain and observing the People's Congress.

Tonight, since we were captives on the ship without land privileges, we had a wonderful BBQ on the pool deck. I ate with the Austrian Food and Beverage Manager, Ernst, who will come to visit us next time he is in Florida. It was very nice, and I enjoyed his company. We know many people in common. Small world!

The dynamics of the passengers and who gets along with whom are getting more and more complex each day. We are waiting for Singapore where about 150 passengers are leaving and about the same number of new ones will board. Many people are now fighting, and the fact that all of them have money does not mean that all of them have good manners or tact. It is great to be a silent observer who, from time to time, takes sides. Many of my on-board friends are Brits and Australians who appreciate an American with an Austrian sense of humor. I am attending Catholic mass on all sea days, and Father Bob sends his best regards. Sister Germaine would be so proud of me.

Again, do not worry, we are safe and feel well protected by the unseen escorts we have to protect us.

CHAPTER 35

PASSENGER STORIES

There was a morgue on the ship because people die at sea all the time. We had two passengers that knew when they boarded that they wouldn't get off the ship alive. I met one young guy, about 40 years old from London, who had cancer of the esophagus. He knew he was not going to make it. He was befriended by the art dealer on board, who had a couple of million dollars worth of art hung all around the ship. Plenty of people were buying art.

The art dealer owned a large ranch in Montana so he told the young man, "Don't worry about it. When you die, I have a nice burial ground for you." And he did. The young man was buried in Montana.

We had another guy who died during dinner one night. He was sitting at a table of ten. While he was eating, all of a sudden, his head hit the plate. The crew was very aware of these happenings, so they kept wheelchairs in every corner of the restaurant. Three guys came, one pushing the wheelchair, and the other two, holding him up. As they pushed him out, they were saying, "Oh, look at

Above photo: Some of my fellow passengers on the SS Mariner.

Mr. Charles. He's drunk again." But the guy was actually dead and being wheeled through the dining room.

When Bill Bates was a cruise director, he got to know a lot of these passengers that take these world cruises. He told me that if I ever travel with Holland America, don't book cabin 223, it's next to the morgue in cabin 221. The room has long shelves where the deceased are held at freezing temperatures, otherwise, they would start to smell.

Bill told me a story about a couple on one trip that had stateroom 223. The couple was complaining to the hotel director, telling him that there was a banging noise coming from the room next to them. They explained that it was very disturbing and asked if they had another room where they could go. They were apologized to and said it was a plumbing problem. A crew member escorted them to the Captain's suite and served some snacks and drinks, while they got the plumber to fix it. So, the "plumber" came down and entered 221 and found that the strap had come loose from all the ship's rocking. Every time the waves went up and down, the head of one of the deceased was hitting the wall. The body was strapped back in again. Bill then informed the passengers that the "plumbing" problem had been fixed, and then put out his hand for a tip and quickly left.

Bill told me another story on a different ship with a different crew. There is always a crew member who is trained to help with burials at sea. The procedure was to take the deceased passenger down to the "potato" level, the bottom where they store the potatoes and onions as it is closest to the water. They performed burials at sea at night while passengers were dining and could not see what was going on. They would place the body on a wooden plank and drape it with the American flag. The priest would be there along with the Captain, the spouse, or any family and friends that are on the trip as well. After a short service, they say their goodbyes, and the crew member then pulled a lever whereby the plank drops the body down into the sea.

On one occasion, an experienced crew member (trainer) was training another crew member (trainee), a Filipino, who had not yet mastered the English language. Meanwhile, the Captain was with the widow and the priest before going down to where her husband was already prepared for burial.

The trainer said to the trainee, "Look at me, when I give you this sign, you pull that lever, and the plank will go up and the body will go down into the water. Do you understand?"

The trainee said, "No."

Once more, the trainer said, "When I do this, you will reach up and pull this level. Then the plank will go up, and the body will slide into the water. Do you understand?"

Again, the trainee said, "No."

The trainer responded, "Now listen, this is the third time. When I do this, you pull this lever, and the body will go into the water. So, did you understand?"

Finally, the trainee responded, "Yes," and pulled the lever.

The body was released into the water with no one there. The Captain, priest and widow were still on top deck, and the body was now gone. So, the trainer went into the store room and grabbed two sacks of potatoes, placed them neatly on the plank, and draped them with another American flag. As soon as everyone came down, they hastened a quick service and dropped the "body" into the water, the widow none the wiser about what had really happened.

I found that a number of people on the ship really expected to die. I was on deck number 10, the top deck. Every state room was the same size, with a balcony, and there were no interior cabins. The difference in price was the deck level and the location. You didn't want to be at the end of the ship over the propellers. I wanted to be on east side, versus the west side, so I would see countryside versus open water all the time.

My next-door neighbor on one side was a lady who was an emergency room physician from North Carolina, but on the other side, was a lady that booked one of the few suites onboard. I believe they had about three or four different kinds of suites, but the remaining 350 rooms were identical. When I boarded the ship in Sydney, I saw this lady being transported off the ship.

I didn't know who she was but she was dressed like a Hollywood star. And she was way up in years. She was put in a limousine along with two young guys. Later we found out that she had been taken to the airport to be flown to Hawaii for cancer treatment. The next time I saw her, she came aboard the ship in Singapore, along with the two young men and now two nurses. I learned later that she was an heir of a well-known Wall Street company, worth billions.

Once she got settled, we exchanged hellos and she said, "Come to my suite at 5:00 for cocktails, and I will tell you what's going on."

So, I did, and she told me that she (about 80 years old) was with her companion (I thought to be maybe 30 years old). Apparently she had homes all over the world, in Paris, Rome, London, New York, and in Australia. This young man was her interior designer and had designed all of her homes but had his design studio in New York where she also lived. Apparently, she didn't get along with members of her family.

I was speaking with her companion, and he told me that one day she said to him, "I want to marry you."

He told me he was gay, and that the other young man was his boyfriend. He further added that he replied to her saying, "Well, this is really a special request, but I can't do that. You are by far my best and biggest client but I have other customers too. And, you know, I just can't give up my business. I'm 28 years old and have my whole life ahead of me. I need to provide for my future."

She then asked him, "How much do you bill a year?"

He said that he told her about $5 million to which she replied, "I'll give you $5 million every year to just be with me."

So, he said, "Well, give me a little time to think about that and talk to my partner."

They did get married, but he didn't give up his studio, which was a thorn in her side.

EMAIL

We had another lecturer, Dr. Barbara Udell, a published lifestyle counselor, psychologist, and very sharp dresser. She has a terrific sense of humor and her style of presentation, with her accent, which is a blend of Miami Beach and Brooklyn, hides her Baltimore background very well. She introduces a different animal in each lecture. So far, she has lectured on the horse, the woodpecker, and the elephant.

As a solo male traveler, one receives constant invitations to dine with other people. By now, I have to keep a journal about who is next. I avoid single ladies for dinner because their competition to be seen with a solo man is ridiculous. Most evenings I will accept invitations from couples. I have met many nice ones, others that are interesting and, of course, those with whom I had to excuse myself before the salad course to return to my stateroom for "medication." Also, I never sit at a table for two. I always request a table for six, so that whomever I'm with, there may be others to keep the conversations going. Last night, there were two ladies among others on my table. One of them had so many face lifts that you could not see her ears any longer, they were hidden behind her head. I left before the salad arrived and went to bed hungry. I am really watching my diet, most of the time by design, and sometimes because of the wrong dining partners. The dynamics are interesting, to put it mildly.

The French ship's doctor is another case. I heard many complaints from all kinds of guests about his rude and arrogant attitude. I experienced some of this myself. He informed me how rude American people are and how poorly educated we are as a nation. I asked him where he was from and he answered, but I could not understand his heavy accent. So I asked again, and his reply was, "If you don't know where this is, go back to school." I asked him if he knows where Dunedin, Florida is. He did not, which provided me the opportunity to suggest additional educational venues for him as well. This was the point in time when I requested for him to return the serum for my allergy shots along with four syringes, which I had shipped ahead. To his credit, he did that without question.

A lady who came to see him for help for her seasickness was told, "What did you expect, you are on a ship, pick up some pills at the front desk." Charge for the consult was $60 U.S. I understand he will be replaced in Hong Kong. Until then, I will have Ricky, my cabin steward, or Dominique, my room service waiter, give me the shots. Other than this man, everyone else is just marvelous.

I awoke at 3:30 a.m. this morning to the sounds of waves crashing against the hull of the ship. I knew it was rough outside my cozy cabin when I noticed whitecaps in my toilet. This morning, the Captain was having breakfast with his life vest strapped on, and the food output from most passengers was greater than the input. Due to the fact that I am not consuming any alcohol, I have not been seasick yet, and also not sick of the sea so far.

EMAIL

I am well and eating very sensibly, which is easy to do since there are so many selections, and I am keeping my portions tiny. Yesterday, I got my head shaved, and people love it. I sold my comb and traded in my shampoo. I abstain from alcohol completely and believe I lost a few pounds.

We are having daily lectures and there are 25 activities and programs scheduled just for this morning all before lunch. There are many more this afternoon. I settled into a routine of paddle ball, bocci ball, and church in the afternoons. Lectures in the morning, little time for journal writing, and mostly declining dinner invitations.

Needless to say, I wish you all were here, I miss you, love you, and can't wait to share all of this in person. Much more detail in the journal. I get so busy at times that I almost forgot what I do for a living. I am scheduled for a TV interview about lifestyle issues and a commentary about the Special Operations Foundation and on, and on, and on.

Some of the interesting people I met on my trip

We had several Gurkhas onboard from Nepal. They are known to be the fiercest fighting force in the world and are considered part of the British military, but have fought for many nations. They don't have guns but carry small curved knives known as khukuri. They often serve to protect embassies around the world. To look at them, you would never know. They were also so nice and were on our ship to protect us against any possible piracy, particularly while we traveled the Straits of Malacca.

Another passenger who had booked the million-dollar Presidential Suite was the owner of a number of cancer hospitals across America. He traveled with his wife, their daughter, and her teacher, his mother-in-law, and two body guards. He, more often than anybody else, invited me to sit at their table to share my stories.

Another passenger, who traveled with his partner, had won a Nobel Prize for cancer research. He lived in San Francisco, taught at the university there, but was originally from Germany. They had a beautiful $20 million home that had caught on fire and burned to the ground with no insurance. So, they were taking this trip around the world for the second time to buy artwork and furnishings for their new home. They booked two state rooms, one for them and the other for all their purchases.

Another couple were two guys from Aventura, Florida near Miami. One was a trust fund baby, also with two suites booked. One for them, and the other held a safe for all of their jewelry, worth hundreds of thousands of dollars. They could only wear all of their jewelry on the ship. I think that if they went through downtown Miami, somebody would cut their arm off for it. I got pretty friendly with them, too.

Dr. Barbara Udell, every day, delivered a lecture about the customs and lifestyle of the next stop or country we were going to visit, as well as what we should do or be sure to see. I always attended her talks, so we became friends quickly. When we arrived in the harbor in Guam, they picked us up by bus to take us to the largest K-mart in the world. Her husband, number five, was an attorney who gave lectures on law. One lecture he gave started with, "If you come home one day, and your spouse has changed her name from Karen to plaintiff, then come and see me for the divorce."

I also met two ladies that lived in Bermuda. Lidge was British royalty and had been married five times. I had heard of her because I had worked at the Southampton Princess in Bermuda. I hadn't met Lidge before, but once I learned she lived in Bermuda, I had a lot to talk to her about. When we arrived, I think in Singapore, she and her friend wanted to go to a male strip club. They asked me to be their escort. I said, "Well, how much do you pay?" I was kidding, of course, and took them. And boy, did they have fun.

I met a Japanese man who told me, in detail, how marriages were arranged in Japan. I was fascinated.

Another lady I met also had two suites. One was for her, and the other was for her wardrobe. Every single day, she wore a different outfit, from top to bottom with matching shoes, hat, jewelry, everything. Another lady I met from South America was an incredibly wealthy woman. Her husband had died, and on the entire trip, an older man was chasing her, but she wanted nothing to do with him.

CHAPTER 36

IT'S A SMALL WORLD

Paulette was not part of the crew but a guest chef who gave cooking lessons to the passengers every day. At night, all the participants had dinner together. In return, she traveled for free. I did not attend many of her classes, but once in a while, she invited me to join them. I liked her, and we did spend some time together. The night we docked in Singapore, Paulette said she had a friend from New York joining her in Singapore for the next segment of the cruise and was going to have a welcome dinner for her. She asked me if I would like to join them. I agreed. Now, before I recount this story, I have to backtrack to my tenure at Innisbrook. I was in charge of everything that had to do with operations, other than golf and tennis, which included food and beverage. Shortly before I left Innisbrook, American Express had raised their fees. We did $50 million worth of business with them, so I asked why. Amex explained that they had to increase our fees because their expenses were going up. I told them that I could not justify that so we would have to terminate our relationship.

Above photo: Paulette and her friend, Loretta, from American Express.

The majority of our clients were Fortune 500 companies with direct billing since everything was generally paid by the company. The individual resort guests, maybe 20% of our business, would use credit cards. I told our front receptionists that when an American Express card was presented, instead of turning them down, I instructed them to ask about their stay, and since they were our valued guests, we would bill them directly. We didn't miss one beat while not accepting American Express. After I left Innisbrook, they continued to not accept American Express for the next five years.

Years later, I had Bon Appétit, and I became the president of the Restaurant Association in Pinellas County, where many of my restaurateur friends were board members as well. One of the issues that came up was that American Express had raised merchant fees for all of the restaurants. So, I shared my story about what I did at Innisbrook, and collectively, they decided to no longer accept American Express.

Now back to my dinner in Singapore with Loretta, who I was sitting next to. I learned that she worked and lived in New York. Since I had lived in New York as well, I asked her where in the city. She replied on 57th Street, which I knew to be the high rent district.

"What do you do for a living?" I asked her.

She replied, "Well, I'm Senior Vice President over credit cards for the hospitality industry. And what do you do?"

I responded, "I come from a small place on the west coast of Florida. I'm sure you've never heard of it. And we have a restaurant and a hotel there."

That's when Loretta asked, "West coast of Florida, where exactly on the west coast?"

Again, I said that I didn't think she had ever heard of Dunedin.

Surprisingly, she said, "Dunedin? I'm very familiar with Dunedin."

Now it was my turn to be surprised and said, "How come?"

"Well," she said, "I'm responsible for American Express credit cards for the whole country. Initially, I dealt with a large resort and then a Restaurant Association there."

I had to be honest. I told her, "I was the bad guy."

She said, "No, no, no, really?"

I told her the whole story and said finally, "Really. I swear to you, it was me."

Fortunately, she didn't hold that against me and was friendly for the remainder of her time aboard.

We had a lovely tour of Singapore given to us by a local detective who told us of the history of the area.

From there we went to Malaysia, where we visited a snake temple where hundreds of snakes lived. Incense was burned inside the temple which was a drug to the snakes and made them move very slowly. A new experience for those of us who dared to go in.

CHAPTER 37
TAJ MAHAL & SEYCHELLES

EMAIL

On Wednesday, I am flying to Agra, India to visit the Taj Mahal. This was a several hour trip across the entire country and back just to see this wonder of the world. We had an interesting lecture about this part of the world in general, and Mahatma Gandhi, in particular. Also, we are being warned about the incredible amount of poverty which we are going to encounter. I thought I had already seen all the poverty there is in this world.

I hope everything is going well at your respective places, and I am looking forward to a nice cold rainy day in a bed that is not moving and where there are no whitecaps in the toilet.

Above photo: Taj Mahal.

EMAIL

Hi my Girlies,

As you know, the Taj Mahal is the most beautiful mausoleum by the Mughal emperor Shah Jahan to house the remains of his wife. It is considered one of the seven wonders of the world. We had a great day visiting this temple of love. It gave me the perfect entree to explain to passengers that the reason my Honey is not on this trip with me is that she is building our temple of love at home. Everyone bought it; me too! It really was a super day. I thought we had seen the worst before, but India's poverty tops other places.

I do think you made the right decision. I am still glad I went, but sometimes it takes all you've got to get through it. I took lots of photos. The cow is sacred here, and some of our guests wanted to know why we are not seeing any McDonald's. As you can see, money, no matter how much you have, does not make you smart.

By this time, you also will note, it is very late, and we set the time back last night by 30 minutes.

Never knew that such a thing existed, but over here, everything seems possible.

Well, the Maharajah sends his love. I had a lot of Yogurt with my Indian airline meal.

Love and kisses, and I miss you; me

EMAIL

Hi everyone,

We came alongside this morning at 8 a.m. and spent the day with Father Bob visiting churches and nude beaches. The beaches are truly out of this world, and we had all the passengers and the crew frolicking in the surf.

We were supposed to sail at 6 p.m. tonight but somewhere last night, we picked up a heavy cable around one of the propellers; therefore, we are stranded on this island and hope to leave tomorrow at noon. It is a law in the Seychelles that no one is allowed to sail after sunset until after sunrise. This still does not explain to me why we have to wait till noon. But such is life at sea.

The place is really very pretty, and the only problem that I see on the horizon is that the menus in the restaurants are in German. This means the Germans are on the way to vacation here, and the place will never be the same. Can't wait to show you the pictures of the Coco de Mar. Our next stop, once we get going, is Africa's east coast.

Mombasa was canceled since there are many riots there, so we are going to Richards Bay. We will be spending 12 hours with the Zulus in their villages, and I will bring many bananas, not for them, but for me because African food scares me even more than the Chinese food I ate.

EMAIL

Hi my Honey and Girlies,

As you know, we had propeller problems that were fixed, and we are now sailing after a 17-hour delay from the Seychelles to Africa during the next four days. Slowly but surely, my sailing days are coming to an end. I will be making a few stops in Africa; Zululand, Rovos Rail through five national game reserves, a few early morning and late-night safaris, and two nights on the train. Then, we end up in Johannesburg to fly back to Cape Town where I will spend the last night on the ship.

This was truly a trip of a lifetime with all the trimmings both positive as well as challenging. We received a few new passengers from Cape Town onto the ship, who have offered to show me around their city. I understand it is wonderful and very inexpensive. If I find more gifts I have not bought yet, I will do so there.

Upon my return home, I will join shoppers anonymous, for sure. Most of the ports in Asia were a shopping frenzy, and I got "Shopper of the Ship" award from the crew. I attend daily lectures on Foreign relations and 5 p.m. mass with Father Bob, who has become a good friend and shore companion.

I can't wait to come home.

CHAPTER 38
SOUTH AFRICA

Our first stop in Africa was to be in Mombasa, Kenya, but there was a revolution there, so we didn't stop. Our next stop was in Durban, South Africa. Many people, even crew members, got off the ship, only to be robbed left and right. A group of 27 of us, however, left the ship to board a Rovos Rail, a special train that was very high class. I had a sitting area and a butler. It was very elegant. The train traveled until midnight each night then stopped hundreds of miles into Africa, in the middle of nowhere. We would sleep until 5:00 a.m. when the jeeps would arrive to take us on safari. We would see different animals, like lions, giraffes and elephants, each day. We did this each of the four nights of the trip, sometimes stopping at sunset, too, for a safari to see the animals feed. We got up close and personal with them.

Our train trip ended in Johannesburg where we boarded a plane to Cape Town. I was definitely the youngest in the group while the mean age of the others was about 82. They ran me ragged. "Peter, I lost my luggage." "Peter, I need a coke." "Peter, I can't find my glasses, teeth, cane." At my age, I was the baby of the gang. We were

Above photo: Rovos Rail stop with the Zulu tribe, along the way to Johannesburg, South Africa.

late arriving back at the ship from our flight so Father Bob and the Captain were anxiously awaiting. They were chiding me about holding the whole ship up.

"I brought 25 people back all alive. Do the math, Father. Add their ages up. Jesus would have been a little boy," I responded. We actually lost one woman on the way never to be seen again. I have no clue where she went.

The ship went on, and crossed the Atlantic and before they reached Brazil, the heiress died on the ship. Her 28-year-old, gay, interior designer husband received $3 billion from her estate.

EMAIL

Hi my Honey and Girlies,

It has been a week since I have gotten off the ship. The first few days when I was in Cape Town, I was very careful, and therefore, lucky not to get mugged, as so many of my friends from the ship and the hotel were. Even on the flight to Europe from South Africa, people were talking about how they were robbed of their money and valuables at knife point. Now I am safe in Bregenz. The weather has been absolutely fantastic, clear blue skies, warm days and very cool nights, dry air and just heavenly. I walk the mountain every day to get back in shape.

Last night, I went to the usual Thursday night exercise course, and had a little bite after that. Everyone, and I mean everyone, is asking about you and sends their regards. This is really a very special place; particularly after having seen the rest of the world. I will meet Stan next week on the first of May, which is a major holiday in Europe, Communist Day. Bubu and Christine went for one week to Spain. Marianne left for three days to Copenhagen. Walter is coming back tomorrow. Gerhadt, Brigitte and Gerard, Alexandra, and all others are here, and everyone wants me to visit and tell them about my adventures. In the meantime, I have all my 900+ photos transferred onto a CD and will share them with everyone; it is easier this way.

Hope all is going well with you. and I am getting really ready to come home because I miss you terribly.

Lots of Love and Kisses; me

Japanese kimono, interchangeable for weddings (as in this picture) and for funerals (other side)

My ryokan bathroom

Founder of the Terracotta Soldiers in Shaanxi province, China

Fine Art dealer and I

My ride on the Great Wall of China

CHAPTER 39

ACHIEVA COMES TO THE RESCUE

On March 20, 2020, we were called to a meeting by the City of Dunedin and informed that we had to close all of our businesses by 3:00 pm that day because of the Covid virus. That gave us two hours to finish feeding our guests, shut everything down and send our employees home until further notice. We were allowed to open once again on May 4th. Of course, this was a nationwide shutdown, not just in Florida.

During that time, we had a skeleton staff in our administrative office. Our controller had, unbeknownst to me, been advised by our current bank that they had Payment Protection Plan (PPP) funding for us. Unfortunately, he did not have a sense of urgency and did not file the paperwork. Because we had been a 47-year customer of our bank, they called our controller again and advised him that if we wanted the PPP funding, he had to complete the paperwork immediately. This was right in the middle of their merger with another large bank.

At some point later, I went to our bank and informed them that we did not have any PPP funding and needed it. That's when I was informed that they did not have any more funding available.

Obviously I was quite disappointed and called Bob Ironsmith, the Director of Economic Development, for the city of Dunedin and told him about our situation.

He said, "You know, I have a good relationship with Gary Regoli, the Chief Executive Officer (CEO,) of Achieva Credit Union. Let me first call and see if Achieva can help you out." He called them and gave them my name as the contact even though I was usually the last person involved with these issues. We had plenty of staff to handle it for us. But in this case, I was the first and only person that Achieva communicated with.

I never got the name of the person that called me, but they did ask that I send the paperwork that was required for PPP funding. At that point, I made sure our controller completed it promptly. Maybe two or three weeks later, I found a message on my office line, that our funding check was ready to be picked up.

Now remember, everything was still closed but Achieva had an emergency drive-up window. So our controller and I drove up to Achieva in Dunedin in his convertible. We drove up to the window and informed the young lady that we were from Bon Appétit Group. To which she replied, "Yes, fine, I have your check right here." She gave us the initial installment that represented a large sum of money. We deposited the funds into our new accounts at Achieva. It was all so effortless.

At this point, I still had never been to, or met anyone at, Achieva though their main office on Achieva Way is in walking distance to my home. After receiving all of the PPP funding, I called the corporate office and introduced myself to whoever answered the phone. I asked them to just relay a message to whoever is in charge of their organization and tell them how much we appreciated what they had done for us. And if I could ever be of any assistance, feel free to call me.

I again called Bob at City Hall and told him that I really wanted to get to know somebody at Achieva. I felt awkward that they gave us so much money so quickly, yet I knew no one there. Bob offered to set up a luncheon and he did. At our lunch, Gary Regoli, the CEO, brought his Chief Business Officer, John Wintermeier, who, at the time, was also the Chair of the Board of Directors for the Dunedin Chamber of Commerce.

Unfortunately, Bob had to leave our lunch early so Gary sat back and for the next two hours, with not one interruption, not one question, he listened to my continuous talking about myself.

Afterwards, he said to me, "You need to write a book."

I told him that I really appreciated the thought but there was no way I could even think about writing a book. I had so many other business obligations and not enough time, nor could I concentrate on one. I am a fireman, I put out fires in the company.

Gary looked at John and said, "Well, we think you should write a book and I think we should pay for it."

I responded that he was very kind to say so and thoughtful to offer to pay for it, but there was no way that would happen, as any book I wrote would be for my girls: Mary, Courtney and Cascy.

Not much later, I got a call from David Oak, Chief Marketing Officer, who said he had heard about our story and how Achieva had helped us.

He asked, "Would you mind sharing your story for our TV commercial?"

I replied that I would be happy to do that. So that's how I came to be on the Achieva commercials, that I believe, ran on all the TV stations in the area for six months. I became quite the celebrity with our Bon Appétit guests for months afterwards when they recognized me from the Achieva ads.

As to re-naming our 1943 Salad, that story goes like this. My spiritual guide is Fr. Bob of St. Francis of Assisi Old Catholic Church, across from the Dunedin City Hall building. He loves that salad so in homage to him, I re-named it the 1942 Salad, his birth year. Well, after Achieva was so kind to us, I again re-named it to the 1942 Achieva Salad. It was a no brainer!

Unbeknownst to me, Gary often came to Bon Appétit and also loved the salad. After we had gotten to know one another, he saw the name change and was pleased. It is my understanding that the 1942 Achieva Salad is ordered for their Board meetings to this day.

Fr. Bob also knows Gary, and we three have had lunch twice. We talked about God and world issues, but not about business. I think very highly of Gary and hope our lunches and friendship continues in the future.

CHAPTER 40

REFLECTIONS

In this book, I wanted to emphasize the time and nurturing I spent over the last 47 years with Bon Appétit restaurant. Each day we thought about how we could make it better, more enjoyable, for not only special events, but also for everyday dining, to meet and exceed our guests' expectations. Over the years, we were approached multiple times to sell Bon Appétit. Last year, we seriously considered and accepted the current owner's offer with only one condition, and that was to maintain every single employee on our payroll after the sale. I pray that they enjoy working with the new owners as much as they enjoyed working with us.

In April 2023, we catered a Celebration of Life reception for 500 guests. All of Belleair was there and as I helped serve the sandwiches, I realized that I knew so many people, and it was all because of Bon Appétit. So many friends in my life have been directly or indirectly a result of Bon Appétit. Guests, purveyors, and city officials have become friends because they dined at Bon Appétit, because they had their own wedding or special events, or attended events, on our second floor.

Above photo: Good friends, Peter and Candy.

I feel so fortunate that I've met so many wonderful people because of my career choice, like the crew from Sound of Music, as one of the founders of the SOCOM Memorial Foundation at MacDill AFB, the Downtown Dunedin Merchant's Association and, being a member of several Boards (Clearwater and Dunedin Chambers, St. Leo's College and Monastery, and the Benedictine Sisters of Florida).

In the early days, and for more than 35 years, I traveled at least twice yearly to Europe, in November to London for the World Travel Market and in the beginning of March to Berlin for the International Tourism Business Exchange. I made hundreds of European and Asian contacts (and collected business cards) that served as preparation for my world cruise. As the years progressed, I started extending these trips to visit my home country of Austria to see friends and business contacts. Over the years, I calculated that I have crossed the Atlantic over 150 times. These trips satisfied my "Fernweh" and kept my roots firmly planted in Dunedin for the past 48 years. And Mary and I have no plans to move elsewhere.

Upon reflection, it was harder to sell Bon Appétit than I thought. But it was time. After nearly 50 years of operating Bon Appétit, I don't have any regrets. It was the right thing to do. Though I miss seeing and meeting the guests, as well as the staff there, every day.

In the long run, Karl was also the right business partner. I don't consider us retired, nor do I want to be. These days, I've given thought to "Fernweh" again. Maybe more travel related activities are in my future.

I hope my daughters learn more about me after reading this book. I think they do what they do with their lives (both are in the medical field) because they saw what I did in mine. Spending so much time at the restaurants and on the other businesses was not a hardship on me because I enjoyed it, walking around, meeting people. They didn't want the same hours or to work every single holiday because we were never closed. And thank goodness for Mary...she never complained.

I have not been a church going person since my days at Melk. What caught my eye about St. Francis of Assisi was that it practiced the Old Catholic faith. It reminded me of my father's religious beliefs and I was curious to learn more about it. I started to attend St. Francis after Fr. Bob celebrated our first Mass in late June, 2019. After the first Mass, we were few in numbers for regular attendance so it was easy to get to know each other. That is how I met Candy Christensen-Barker, who was a close friend of Fr. Bob's. That Christmas, we decided to donate food to Dunedin Cares, a local food pantry, which Candy handled on behalf of the church. When she came by my office to present me with my contribution bill, we started to talk about her background. This was the time of the pandemic which hit our business hard in recruiting qualified team members. As an HR Consultant, I asked Candy to help us recruit over the next year, which she did. As a result of working so closely with Candy during 2020, Mary and I formed a deep friendship with her. Mary and Candy are now "sisters." At some point, I told her that our girls wanted me to write a book about my life, so she offered to help. And she did. Without her, this book would never have happened.

Starting in early 2022, Candy spent hours recording my memories, asking questions and then writing this book. I truly believe this was divine intervention. God will put the right people in your life when you need them. Candy calls them her angels. She is one of mine. I am incredibly grateful for her collaboration in helping me fulfill Courtney and Casey's wishes.

BIOGRAPHY

PETER WERNER KREUZIGER was born in Vienna, Austria but immigrated to the United States in December 1964 after being educated at the Benedictine Abbey of Melk in Austria and then completing a three-year hotel apprenticeship. Peter is a graduate of the School of Hotel Administration at Cornell University, after which he opened, managed and was affiliated with hotels and restaurants in North America, Bermuda and Acapulco.

In 1976, Peter and his business partner, opened the Bon Appétit restaurant on St. Joseph's Sound in Dunedin, Florida which was sold in November 2022. He is the President and CEO of Leisure Management Services, Inc., which owns and operates Café Alfresco, Florida Beach Services, and other real estate holdings in the Tampa Bay area.

Peter is a founding member of the Downtown Dunedin Merchant's Association, the founding President of the United States Special Operations Command Memorial Foundation, and a member of The American Committee on Foreign Relations. He has also been on the Board of Directors of the Clearwater and Dunedin

Chambers of Commerce, and is a licensed Captain with the U.S. Coast Guard.

He lives in Dunedin, Florida with his wife, Mary Kreuziger (nee Miller), with whom he shares two grown daughters, Courtney and Casey, along with two pugs, Baxter and Ali.

ACKNOWLEDGMENTS

My first thanks go to my wonderful daughters, Courtney and Casey, who have hinted for many years that I needed to write a book. Without their request, I don't think I would have come up with the idea by myself.

A forever thank you to my wife, Mary, who has supported me for the last 45 years in all that I have done. Being the wife of a restaurateur and hotel owner, has often been a lonely one. You have single-handedly raised our girls to be the kind, thoughtful and strong women that they are. You always took care of me so that I could devote my time and efforts to running the businesses which often meant travel and my time away from home. I am eternally grateful for your support.

I am grateful to Candy Christensen-Barker who spent countless hours recording my memories and then transcribed and re-phrased my words to create this book. Her enthusiastic offer to help me, laugh at my stories, encourage me, and keep us going is very much appreciated.

To my publisher, Lil Barcaski, who worked so many hours to put our written words in some semblance of order, to come up with a title, and who also laughed at my stories that encouraged me that this was a project I could be proud of, I thank you.

Karl Riedl, my business partner and my friend, thank you for over 50 years of partnership and friendship. Without your support, many of my personal and professional accomplishments would never have happened.

To all of our former associates of Bon Appétit, thank you for your hard work and dedication that made this restaurant the most popular and successful restaurant in the Tampa Bay area as recognized by so many awards over the last 47 years. I wish you all continued success in your endeavors.

To our current associates of Café Alfresco and Florida Beach Services, thank you for your continued dedication to service excellence and good food.

To the City of Dunedin, and its leadership, for being so welcoming and supportive of all of our businesses and sharing in my vision to help Dunedin grow as a great vacation destination, as well as a desired community to live in.

Being a founding member and the first president of the United States Special Operations Command Memorial Foundation (SOCOM) has been one of my most cherished achievements. Together with community leaders, we fulfilled our mission to build a million-dollar memorial at MacDill Air Force Base in Tampa, Florida, to honor those quiet professionals who have paid with their lives, in both war and peace.

Gary Regoli, thank you for listening to my life story, and thinking it was so interesting that I needed to write a book. Your statement and kind offer got me working on it.

To my dear friends, too many to name, but in my heart. Thank you all for your friendships, for eating at our restaurants, staying in our hotel, for donating to my important causes, for traveling with me to Europe, for giving me good advice, for being a listening ear, and for the many other ways you have proven your friendship, I humbly thank you.

To Father Bob, for being my spiritual guide in all the really important things beyond this life.

To the over 11 million dining guests that have supported Bon Appétit and Café Alfresco over the last several decades, I appreciate your patronage. Walking in and seeing you at our tables has given me so much pleasure, deep satisfaction, and eternal gratefulness that I have been able to follow my dreams and have had the best career ever!

265

that I have been able to follow my dreams and have had the best career ever!

Printed in the USA
CPSIA information can be obtained
at www.ICGtesting.com
JSHW010732121023
49936JS00001B/1